A GIRL'S BEST FRIENDS

CREATIVE JEWELRY DESIGN

gestalten

PREFA

Akong
London,
see pp. 20, 24,
25, 44, 45

In 2007, clay-covered shells dating back 82,000 years
were found in Morocco. They are thought to be the oldest
known form of human adornment, as well as proof of man's
innate ability to think symbolically. In the same year, Ted Noten's
RataSmile—a rat holding a diamond in its mouth, encased
in a block of acrylic and outfitted with a trolley—was presented in
Venice on the occasion of the Venice International Film Festival
and titled *Wearable Art for Stars*. The acrylic-cast creations of this
Dutch designer are exhibited at museums and sold at international fairs, auctions and galleries for thousands of dollars. At the same
time and for under $100, one can modify a cellular pattern using
a Creative Commons online applet developed by design team
Nervous System, who will then 3D print the pattern in nylon or
stainless steel as a one-of-a-kind ring, and send it to the purchaser
anywhere in the world.

Whether high or lowbrow, ready-made or carefully crafted,
conventional or conceptual, jewelry has been a part
of human culture for millennia. As bodily adornment it has served
so many purposes: as an object of ritual, as a functional element,
as a demonstration of status, as currency, as a sign of sentiment on
the part of the giver, or as an aesthetic statement on the part
of the creator or wearer. Jewelry tells stories of wealth and admi-
ration, of identity, or even of social critique. Throughout history,
jewelry has been collected, traded, sold, stolen, bequeathed, inher-
ited, exhibited, or discarded, its value shifting according to those
who handle it.

CE

Atelier Ted
Noten,
see pp. 17–19,
28, 29, 38, 39

Gitte Nygaard,
see pp. 66, 227

Jewelry today is described and categorized in any number of ways, many of which incorporate aspects of one another. While some terms differentiate according to the quality of materials, such as fine jewelry vs. costume jewelry, other definitions look more to the mode of jewelry production, such as commercial or mass-produced collections vs. limited series or one-of-a-kind pieces. Studio jewelry can also be costume or fine jewelry, depending on the materials its creator has chosen to use. Although the world of high jewelry boasts some fantastical creations, its use of rare and precious gemstones remains in the foreground; production factors such as cost and time can further narrow the margin for experimentation.

A *Girl's Best Friends* presents a survey of new works within the world of contemporary studio jewelry, which is a rapidly evolving multifaceted field. Also known in the English language as artistic/artisanal/auteurist jewelry—or simply contemporary jewelry—studio jewelry may be understood as a certain approach to the craft, a practice that unites skilled craftsmanship with individual vision. Contemporary studio jewelry pushes boundaries, engaging in direct or implicit dialogue with the history, value, and use of adornment and its relation to the body. It is treasured more for its concept and originality than for the market value of its materials.

The origins of contemporary studio jewelry may be found in the late 19th century arts and crafts movement that originated in England in reaction to industrialization, a movement which advocated a return to traditional artisanry. French art nouveau

4

Bless,
see pp. 108,
109

Naoko Ogawa,
see
pp. 85, 194,
195

designer René Lalique is also considered a forerunner, as he revo-lutionized the art of jewelry by prioritizing his own vision and virtuosity over precious materials and convention. Contemporary studio jewelry is also the offspring of the modernist jewelry movement, in which jewelers breaking with the mainstream looked to the fine arts for inspiration. Building on the Bauhaus manifesto that artisan and artist are one in the same, the notion of wearable art emerged in opposition to mere ornament, and secured its place in museums and galleries. The second half of the 20th century saw the development of a critical discourse surrounding contemporary studio jewelry, with a vocabulary informed and influenced by other artistic and philosophical arenas.

Contemporary studio jewelry now finds itself at the nexus of art, fashion and design. Its practitioners realize their visions with conventional and nonconventional materials, precious and common, natural and synthetic—and also with the techniques used to manipulate these. While many artists have trained as traditional goldsmiths, others find their way to jewelry from neighboring disciplines, such as fine arts, fashion, architecture, and design, blurring the lines between these disciplines as their experience from the one nourishes their craft of the other. The development of new and increasingly cost-efficient technologies, such as rapid prototyping, has not only introduced innovative materials and working methods to the field, but has also enabled designers to explore new formal possibilities, while concurrently raising issues of reproducibility, uniqueness, and accessibility.

Access and exposure to contemporary studio jewelry cannot be ignored as a factor in its growing recognition and popularity, as well as in its expansion into other disciplines. Galleries and international fairs have been the mainstay behind the widespread exposure and collecting of contemporary studio jewelry.

Fairs such as Schmuck in Germany and SOFA in the United States have been joined by the 2009 relaunch of Collect at the Saatchi Gallery in London, as well as Object Rotterdam, and Design Miami/Basel, which in the last few years have exhibited contemporary studio jewelry with the same reverence as design collectibles. The catwalk as well has long been a friend of contemporary studio jewelry, either as fashion accessories or as fashion in its own right.

The internet also plays a major role, with the prevalence of artist websites, craft forums, and the multiplication effect through blogs. Online shops, with their streamlined channels of distribution, also open up the market to an expanding global community of aficionados.

Despite the economic crises that have marked the first decade of the new millennium, the prevalence of independent boutiques, and even retail stores marketing niche products such as one-of-a-kind or limited-run jewelry series by contemporary jewelry designers, seems to be on the upswing, as consumers look to quality instead of quantity, even as what they wear often provokes and undermines the very market system that sustains it.

The jewelry documented in this book has been loosely grouped according to five playful "muses" matched to categories, describing more of a sensibility than a strict line of thought. The various works utilize a vast array of materials and technical approaches to invoke these five sensibilities, in concept and/or design. Yet just as they seek to transcend categorization and conventional definitions of jewelry, here too, there is ample room for interpretation and crossover.

LIZ opens the book with works that point to a dialogue of GLAMOUR and preciousness with regards to concept, material, design—or all of the above. Nicole Akong of Akong London pp. 20, 24, 25, 44, 45, for example, who was born in the West Indies and is now based in London, invokes a sense of tribal bling with her luxurious

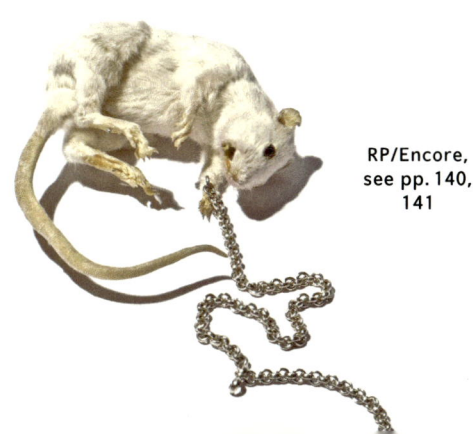

RP/Encore,
see pp. 140,
141

statement necklaces composed of chains, pompoms, and ribbons with golden leaves and crystals. The draping necklaces are designed to embellish clothing as much as the body of the wearer, blurring the line between jewelry and fashion. In a similar vein, the acrylic bags by Dutch designer Ted Noten [pp. 17–19, 28, 29, 38, 39] are multilayered narratives. Posh designer handbags are elongated with acrylic blocks that preserve and showcase items from the scenes of sensational, fictitious crimes: jewels, drugs, and weapons. Rendering the objects useless as individual elements heightens their symbolic value as a whole.

T he works ascribed to **AUDREY** are significantly more **MINIMAL** in nature. Danish designer Gitte Nygaard [pp. 66, 227] engages a dialogue with fine jewelry by utilizing a different incarnation of the substance of diamonds: coal. Her simple *Button* pendant, a piece of sustainably sourced Japanese Binchotan coal (said to have healing properties) attached to a silver chain, opens up a conversation about man and nature, and the roles of jewelry as ornament, accessory and talisman. Also minimal are the *Along with you* partner rings by Japanese designer Naoko Ogawa [pp. 85, 194, 195], which when seen from the outside look like simple gold rings. However, a small notch on the inside of each ring is a constant tactile reminder of the other wearer. The discreet intervention results from the slight overlapping of two rings.

L ADY G pushes the **CONCEPT** of the jewelry pieces into the foreground. The *Cable Jewellery* by German design team Bless [pp. 108, 109] takes those everyday objects that are usually rather hidden and elevates them to fashion objects by adding further elements such as feathers, fur and pearls. Bless hearkens coyly to couture's principle of "custom made," as well as to the status of the artist as alchemist, by inviting buyers to submit their own cables for transformation into jewelry. Also demonstrating conceptual insight is the 24 karat gold ring by Danish designer Kim Buck [pp. 12, 104, 105, 161, 164] titled *Gold, Jewellery, Gold, Jewellery, Gold…* Due to

Aoi
Kotsuhiroi,
see
pp. 128–131

Kim Buck,
see pp. 12,
104, 105, 161,
164

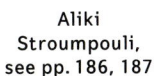

Aliki
Stroumpouli,
see pp. 186, 187

Denise Julia
Reytan,
see pp. 13,
31, 148–151,
188–190

its inherent softness it is designed to return to its original shape as a lump of gold over the course of wear.

Driven by the dark beauty of nature, life and death, **IVY** points to jewelry with a more **GOTHIC** sensibility. While couture may have its mink stoles, Reid Peppard of RP/Encore pp. 140, 141 uses the preserved bodies of dead rats, ravens, and squirrels along with metal cast skeletal elements in her bracelets, necklaces, brooches, and headpieces. Creatures otherwise considered to be vermin become reminders of the troubled fascination man has for nature. In another gothic flavor, the dark eroticism of traditional Japanese kinbaku rope bondage is referenced in the works of Aoi Kotsuhiroi pp. 128–131 in jewelry that is a lyrical blend of adornment and performance.

Finally, **POP** icon **CYNDI** showcases a celebration of color and pastiche. For her *Accessorize Recycling Project,* Greek designer Aliki Stroumpouli pp. 186, 187 playfully composed elements culled from past collections of a costume jewelry company she worked for into new, one-off creations. Similarly, the colorful neckwear by German designer Denise Julia Reytan pp. 13, 31, 148–151, 188–190 celebrates the leveling of high and low culture. Her creations combine diverse materials such as stones, beads, and found objects that she harmonizes by casting them in silicone.

While the featured works by over one hundred artists have been united by the publication of A *Girl's Best Friends*, they remain distinct in their appearance, their materials, and in how and why they are made—variables that influence one another in the constant play between form and content that characterizes contemporary studio jewelry as a genre. By placing the pieces in the spotlight, this book ultimately celebrates the immediate and visceral nature of jewelry that lies at its essence, and whets our appetite for more to come.

LIZ
~GLAMOUR

1

PATRIK MUFF
"KÄFERRINGE"[1]
Skulls, flaming hearts, and mythical creatures are
some of the symbols that comprise the visual vocabulary used by designer Patrick Muff in his bold and
ornate rings, pendants, and bracelets.—18 karat gold,
white and colored brilliants—

"ASPEN"[2]
Ethnic bracelet: clasp in sterling sliver, coral; *Skull*
ring with movable jaw: white gold 750|000, approx.
1.9 karat of pavé, white diamonds; Baron ring: sterling
silver, moonstone—

KIM BUCK
"COPY?"

Kim Buck fashions wearable pieces that offer
reflections on the form, meaning, and material of
jewelry. His pieces, often made of gold, silver,
and even metallic foil, reference conventional design
concepts while simultaneously deconstructing
the same conventions.—750 gold—

DENISE JULIA REYTAN
"REVOLUTION BROOCH 2"

Denise Julia Reytan might be considered a modern
bricoleur, as she combines a potpourri of found
objects into colorful statement necklaces that she calls
"poems on the body." Regardless of their market
value, the diverse objects are equal in their symbolic
value for their creator, who "harmonizes"
them in materiality and color through silicone or
silver casting.—Silver, fine gold plated—

JOOMI LIM
"LOVE HURTS"

Design duo Joomi Lim and Xavier Ricolfi present an upscale take on punk rock and tribal motifs. Edgy elements such as spikes, studs, or chunky chain are reworked in precious metals and playfully combined with pearls, crystals, and fringe.—Swarovski crystal, pearls/brass chain, brass spikes dipped in matte gold and antique rhodium—

THE OPULENT PROJECT
"COSTUME COSTUME COCKTAIL RING"

Founded by Meg Drinkwater and Erin Gardener, TOP seeks to subvert mainstream preconceptions regarding value in material culture. For this series exploring costume jewelry, inexpensive costume cocktail rings found in China were cast entirely in silver. The ostentatious design of the original rings is further exaggerated by stacking them in sets of two and three.—925 silver—

NOEMI KLEIN
"GLACIER/ROCK RINGS"

Influenced by gothic romanticism, avant-garde culture and "ephemeral imagery of life and death," Noemi Klein casts and elements of nature in gold and silver, resulting in finely detailed rocks, twigs and shards of wood that are worked into necklaces, rings and earrings.—Sterling silver, 22 karat gold plating—

GÖRAN KLING
"SIGNET RING BRACELET"
For his *Signet Ring Bracelet*, Göran Kling reproduced
signet rings of recognizable jewelry houses in
gold-plated brass and repurposed them as a bracelet—
making a witty nod to the market of mass-
produced replicas as well as to the allure of bling.
—Gold-plated brass—

ATELIER TED NOTEN
"ICE NECKLACE"

In much of his work with acrylic, Ted Noten embalms objects of desire, nostalgia or emotional value, removing them from the everyday and transforming them into icons, showcased in the context of jewelry.—Necklace in acrylic—

ATELIER TED NOTEN

"ICEPICK BAG" [1]

Made from posh designer handbags extended by
a block of acrylic, Ted Noten's acrylic bag series
including the iconic *Icepick Bag* and the numerous
Lady K Bags present multilayered narratives of
sensational, fictitious crimes filled with jewels, drugs,
and weapons.—Icepick, gold ring, synthetic
diamonds, cocaine, textile, cultivated pearls—

"LADY K BAG NR. 4" [2]

—Bag, engraved and heavily gold-plated gun and
bullet, textile—

STUDIO ULI BUDDE
"UNFOLD"

The *Unfold* necklace is based on designer Uli Budde's examination of the round brilliant cut developed by Marcel Tolkowsky in 1919. Paper models of the iconic diamond shape in various stages of unfolding were rapid-prototyped in wax and then cast in gold. The interior of the pendant maintains the rough marks of its laser-sintered mold, while the exterior is polished.—18 karat gold—

AKONG LONDON
"GOLD LEAF BRACELET"

See description on p. 25—Aluminium chain, opalite, crystals, gold-plated leaves—

JOOMI LIM
"QUEEN BEE"

See description on p. 14—Swarovski crystal / brass chain dipped in oxidized brass—

MARQUIS & CAMUS
"BLACK CHANDELIER NECKLACE"

Marquis & Camus, founded by designer Sarah Kang, hearkens back to a more romantic era while remaining rooted in the present. Vintage elements such as chandelier crystals, charms, and buttons are brought together with contemporary elements including metallic chains, hand-died ribbons, rhinestones, and pearls to create whimsical creations with a classic twist.—Vintage earring and chandelier crystal, smokey quartz and onyx, rhinestone chain, mixed chain—

JOOMI LIM
"TRIBAL FESTIVAL"

See description on p. 14—Swarovski crystal/brass skull & spikes dipped in rhodium

HENRIETTE LOFSTROM
"BLACK TRIANGLE BREAST PLATE"

With an aesthetic that draws inspiration from ancient civilizations, mysticism, and futuristic fantasies, the jewelry by Henriette Loftstrom reflects notions of symmetry, geometry, and the multiplication of form.—Stainless steel—

PIA ALEBORG
"TAKE YOUR SEAT!"
With the jewelry series *Take Your Seat!* Pia Aleborg attempts to convey the tension between the characteristics of the famous Chesterfield sofa and the powerful physical sense she experiences when sitting in one.—Leather, rivets, horse hair, plywood—

SASKIA DIEZ
"DIAMOND
AND PAVÉ BRACELETS"
Classic cuts normally used for precious gemstones
are enlarged and transferred onto massive bronze
or solid colored glass for this bracelet series by Saskia
Diez.—Glass, bronze, nylon—

AKONG LONDON
"CHAIN HARNESS" [1]
"GOLD LEAF NECKLACE" [2]
The opulent statement necklaces and cuffs by Nicole
Akong of Akong London are characterized by bold
combinations of colors and materials, such as gold and
silver chains, feathers, pom-poms, and fur trim along
with semi-precious gemstones. The attention-grabbing
pieces are designed to embellish clothing as
much as the wearer's body.—Aluminium chain,
opalite, gold-plated leaves—

NOON PASSAMA
FOR CAPARA, SPRING/ SUMMER 2012

The ironic formalism of artist Erwin Wurm served as inspiration for the collection created by Noon Passama for Capara. Two classical chain forms are enlarged, distorted, and combined in a variety of colors and sizes.— 1: Electroformed copper, car paint—2: Electroformed silver (18 karat gold-plated)—

ATELIER TED NOTEN
"HAUNTED BY 36
WOMEN – AVONDVLINDER"

For his recent collection *Haunted by 36 Women*, Ted Noten created pieces based on 36 female archetypes. Assembling found objects in order to describe them, he used rapid prototyping to transmute the creations into perfect scale models in a variety of sizes and materials. The final piece of each archetype is a unique creation, cast in solid gold.—Rings: titanium black; Ring: 18 karat gold—

GÖRAN KLING
"REPLICA 3" & "REPLICA 1"
A homage to the classic timepiece as well as "cheap knockoffs," Göran Kling's *Replica* collection pieces resemble wristwatches, but without the clock. Instead, the designer works in pendants that more or less reference the watch face that they replace.—Gold-plated brass—

DENISE JULIA REYTAN
"T1MEPEACE CHRONO"
Denise Julia Reytan encourages wearers to forget
about time with her *T1MEPEACE* collection. The
stainless steel and faceless watch skeletons are gold,
silver or platinum-plated, and can be bent to fit
the wrist as needed.—100% nickel-free stainless steel,
fine gold-, silver- or ruthenium-plated—

INA.SEIFART
"UHRENARMBAND"
The Timeless Bracelet by Ina Seifart is a simple
yet compelling counterfunctional intervention.
A gold-plated steel watchband holds not a watch face
but a sleek rectangular link that reveals and
frames the wearer's skin beneath it.—Gold-plated
steel—

ALYSON FOX
"OBJECT 3"

The creations of Alyson Fox offer subtle commentary
on design as well as on society. With her *Objects*,
a limited edition collection of bronze-cast pins made
from found materials, she explores the notion of
weapons made from everyday things.—Cast bronze—

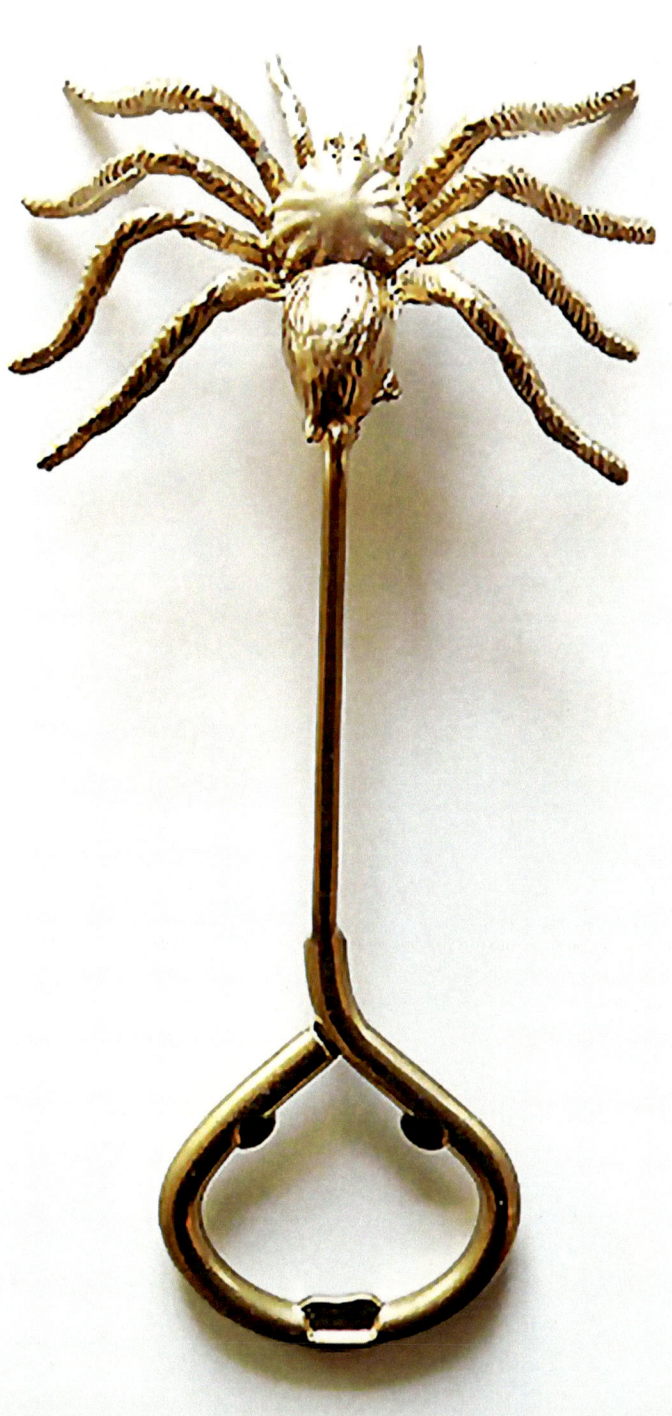

1

2

MIRIT WEINSTOCK

"GOLD SHADOW STATEMENT NECKPIECE" [1]

Natural feathers taken from shuttlecocks used for the game of badminton have been a central material in the jewelry by Mirit Weinstock. Coated in silver through electroforming, or gold plated, or oxidized, the feathers are presented alone or else combined with flowers, knitting, or pleats for a playful and feminine effect.—Shuttlecock feathers, plated silver and gold, brass—

"HALF DIPPED SHUTTLECOCK NECK PIECE" [2]

—Shuttlecock feathers, plated silver, silk, gold—

"SHUTTLECOCK HAIR JEWELRY" [3]

—Shuttlecock feathers, plated silver and gold—

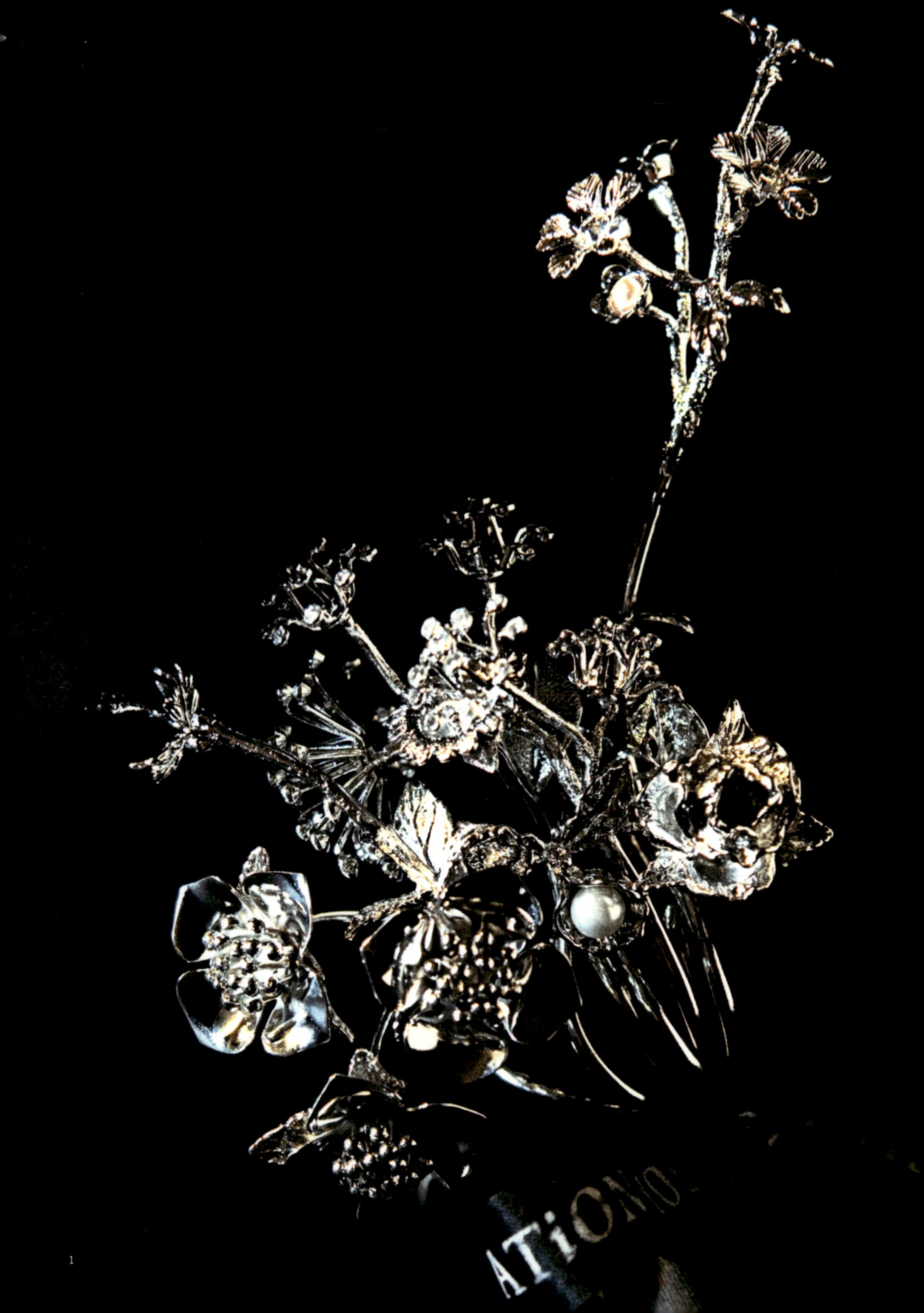

1

2

YOSHIKO CREATION PARIS
"FOR YOU" [1]
Under the label Yoshiko Creation Paris, Yoshiko
Kajitani creates avant-garde, one-off pieces that have
been embraced by couture. Her *Renaissance* collection
features ornate jewelry dedicated to the parts of the
body, and also the notion of rebirth.—Brass—

BIJULES
"ROCK RING" [2]
The renegade creations by Bijules founder Jules Kim
have gained cult status for their unique combination
of jewelry and art, classicism and punk, decadence
and sophistication. Motifs such as snakes, bird skulls,
rocks and bones associated with memento mori
appear in delicate arrangements of sculpted metal and
gems; offering a study in contrasts and the thrill of
contradiction.—Silver—

ATELIER TED NOTEN
"DESIGN ICON RINGS"
Presented in an elegant collector's box, these 25 signet
rings of sterling silver, designed by Ted Noten,
are engraved with icons from the design world, such
as Gerrit Rietveld's *Red and Blue Chair*,
Philippe Starck's *Juicy Salif* lemon squeezer, and the
Cartier *Trinity* ring.—Sterling silver—

1

2

H A N N A H   M A R T I N
"VINCENT'S FACET SIGNET" [1]
A fusion of decadent luxury and cutting edge design, Hannah Martin's
jewelry collections for men are each accompanied by a narrative
describing the figure that inspired her collection. The *Vincent* collection
by Hannah Martin tells the story of an underground Russian
oligarch at home in the ranks of London society. Referencing Russian
imperial and communist iconography, bold facet shapes sculpted
by radiating graphic lines are traditional in style yet modern in detail.
—18 karat yellow gold, hand-cut black onyx, diamond—

"VINCENT'S EMPTY SOVEREIGN" [2]
—18 karat yellow gold, hand-cut blue-black sapphires—

IRENE WOOD
"AUTUMNAL"
Jewelry designer and painter Irene
Wood uses round and faceted
wooden and acrylic beads in
monochromatic and colorful combinations to craft chunky, collar-
like necklaces inspired by
textiles as well as ancient
Greco-Roman and Egyptian
jewelry.—Painted wood—

AKONG LONDON
"CRYSTAL TASSEL COLLAR"[1]
See description on p. 25—Chain, crystals, tassel trim,
velvet ribbon—

"BRIGHT
POM POM NECKLACE"[2]
—Chains, velvet ribbon, pom pom trim, cord—

EVERT NIJLAND
NECKLACE 'ROCOCO' OUT OF THE NATURAE SERIES

Evert Nijland draws inspiration from the interpretation of nature by artists from the Renaissance and Baroque periods. He works within various disciplines of the applied arts in order to bring together a variety of materials in his creations, such as handwoven linen, porcelain, bronze, iron, and glass beads.—Porcelain, handwoven linen—

1

2

3

4

TERHI TOLVANEN
"SHADOWS
AND SILHOUETTES" [1]
Terhi Tolvanen brings natural materials such as
coral, wood, agate, and quartz together with
silver, silk, and even cement in poetic, sculptural
jewelry that comments on the relationship

1

2

3

T E R H I   T O L V A N E N
"G O U T T E S" [1]
—Wood, labradorite, silver, textile—

"G R A P P E" [2]
—Amethyst, wood, silver, textile—

"C E R I S I E R" [3]
—Wood, rose quartz, gold—

"S H A D O W S
A N D S I L H O U E T T E S" [4]

4

AUD

~ MINIMAL

REY

1

SASKIA DIEZ
"FINE NECKLACES" [1]

The *Fine* collection by Saskia Diez consists of basic
jewelry items made from silver and 18 karat
yellow gold in two different chain structures: one
of small rings, one of small squares. Necklaces
and bracelets all have the same fastening structure
so they can be easily combined—lengthened or
layered according to whim. The rings are also flexible,
like miniature necklaces for the finger.—18 karat
gold, sterling silver—

"SILVER FINE
WILD NECKLACE" [2]
—Sterling silver—

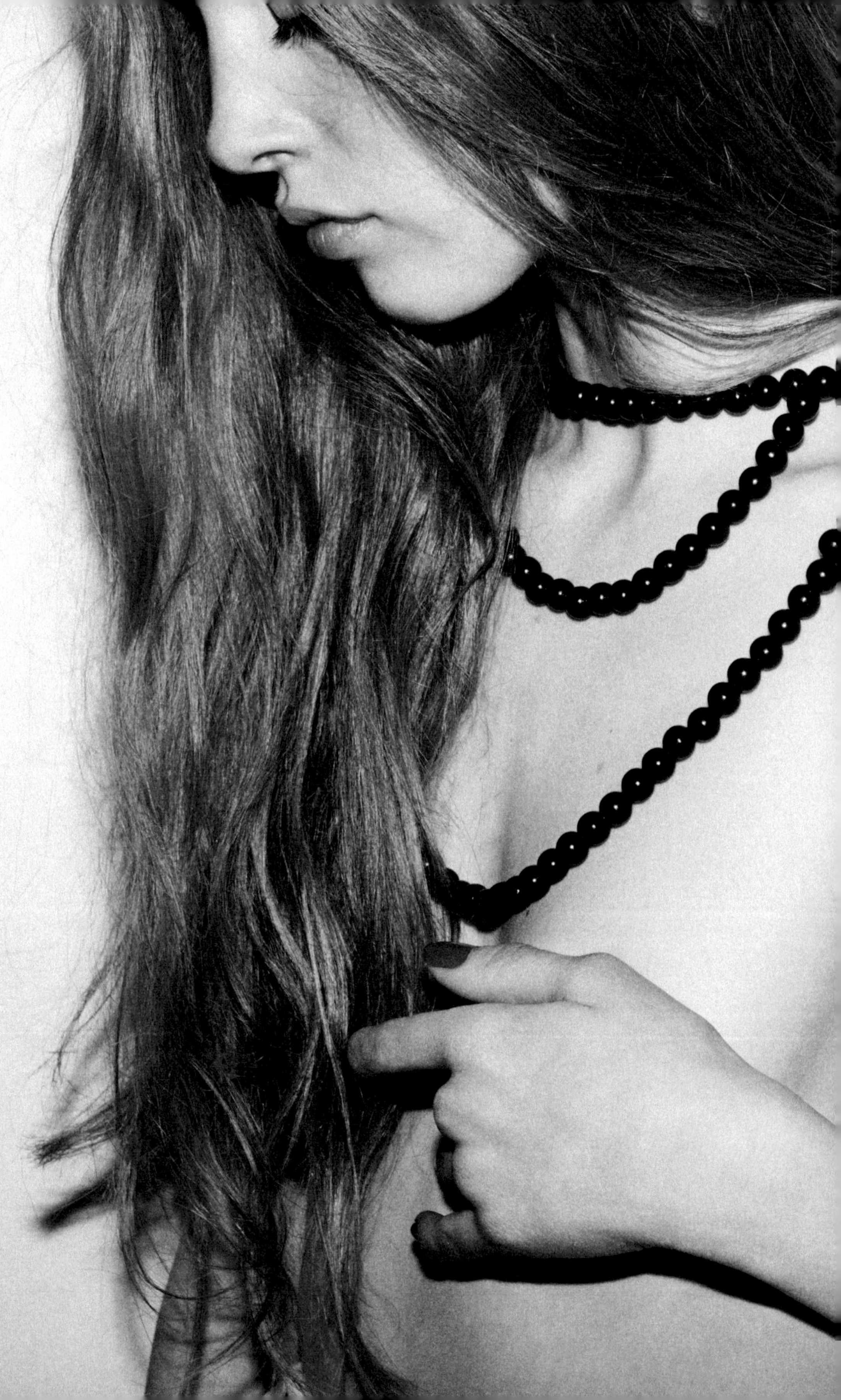

SASKIA DIEZ
"BLACK LACE CAPE"
The *Lace* series by Saskia Diez
blurs the line between clothing
and jewelry. Strands of lacquered
wooden beads come in four
different geometrical patterns
and are named according to the
familiar clothing pieces that
describe their purpose: collar, cape,
shoulder, and neckpiece.—Lacquered wood beads, elastic nylon,
engraved sterling silver label—

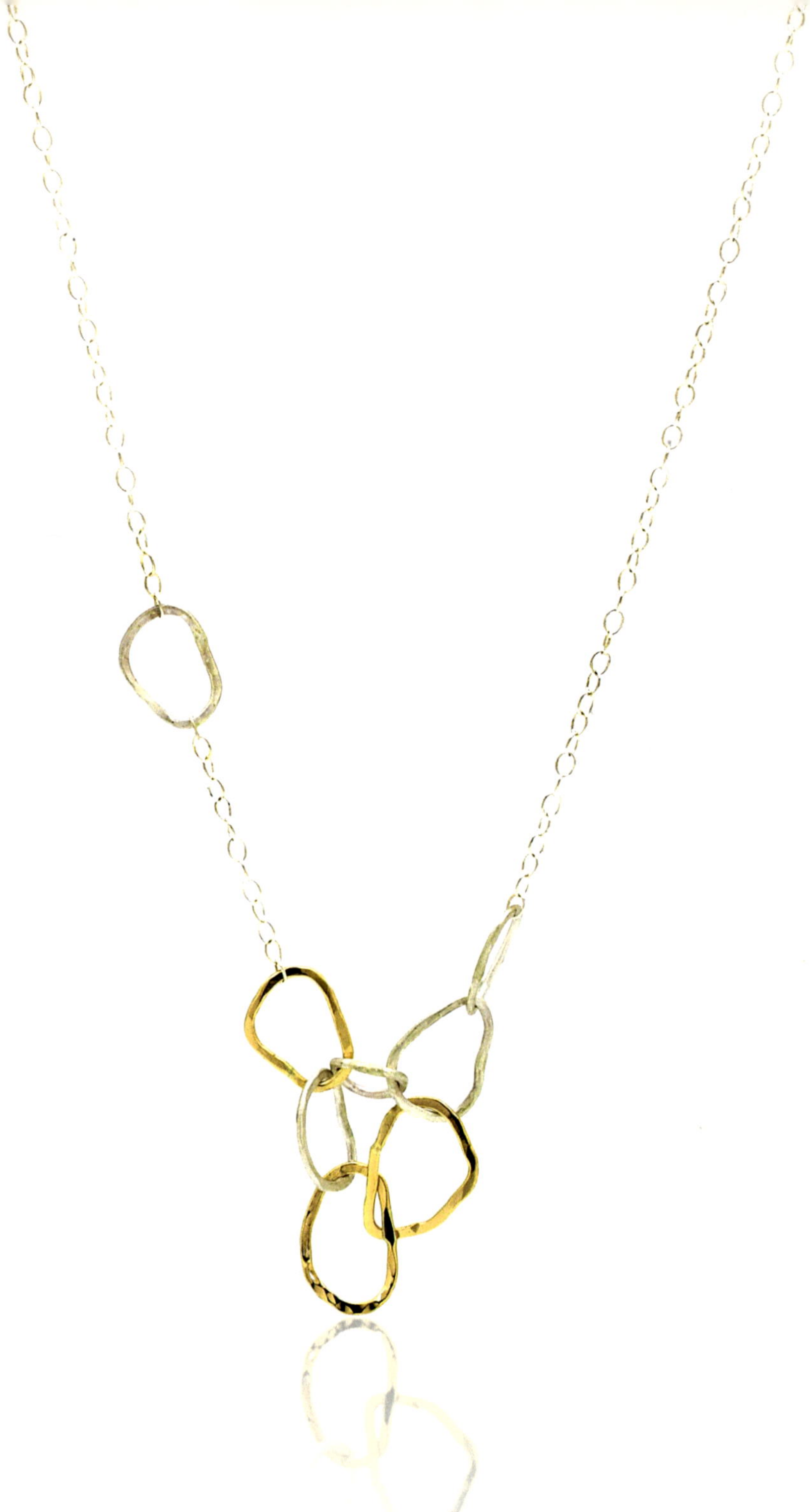

1

MARJORIE VICTOR
"PUZZLE NECKLACE" [1]
Marjorie Victor combines various hand-textured, organic shapes into grace-
ful, asymmetrical creations that arrange themselves in delicate
balance with the movements of the wearer.—Sterling silver, 14 karat goldfill—

"TIERED PUZZLE NECKLACE" [2]
—Sterling silver, 14 karat yellow, 14 karat rosegold—

2

ARMOR JEWELRY
"ABEE" [1]

Deftly linking the worlds of fashion and jewelry,
Sandee Shin for her label Armor Jewelry makes
draping, chained creations that are strong as well as
feminine. The various chain sizes and textures
are combined to best accentuate the part of the body

2

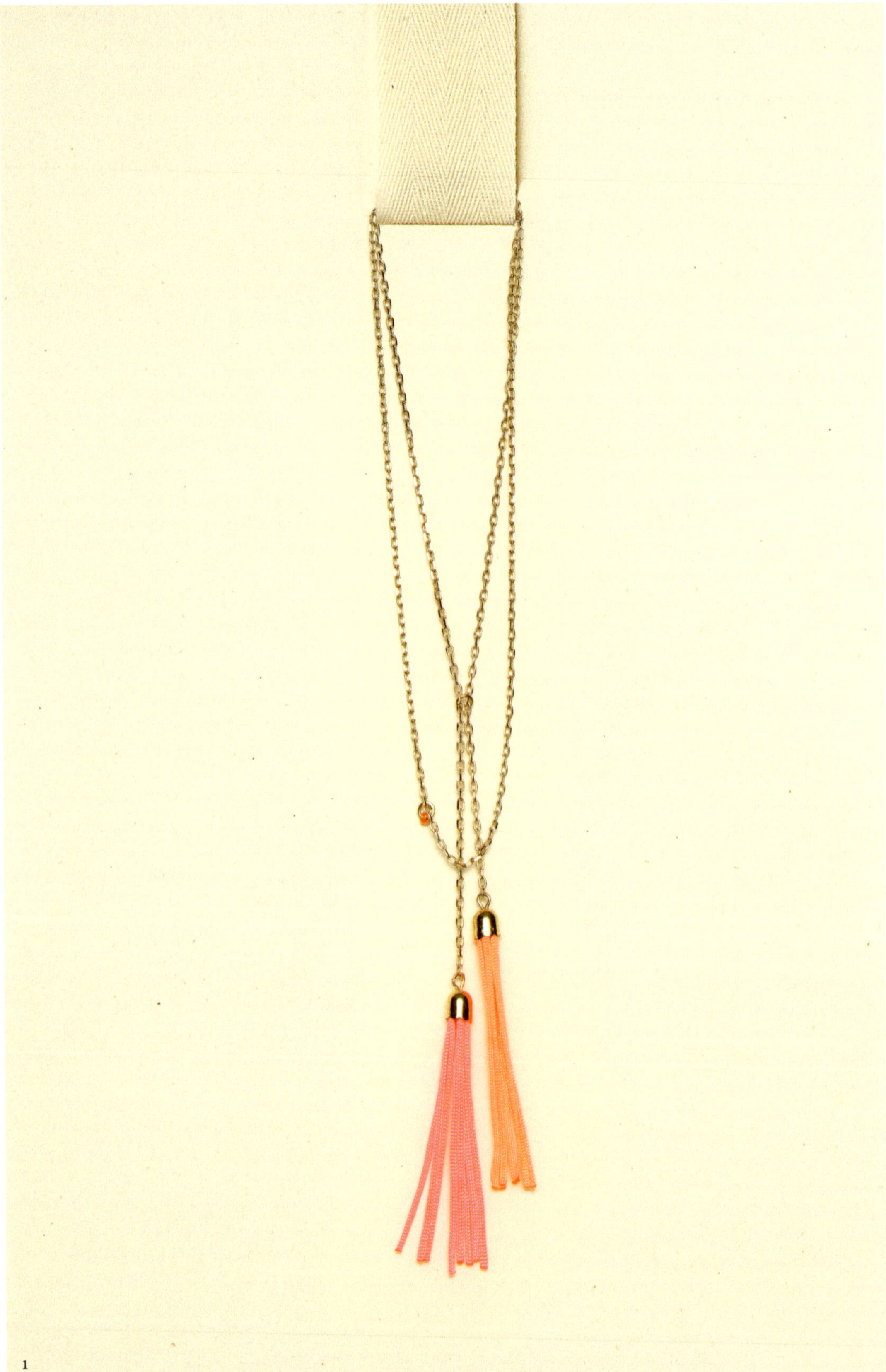
1

2

3

5

4

TURINA.JEWELLERY
"S11/2.1" [1]

The *Now* collection by Sandra Turina features playful, minimalistic studies in fashion detailing. A few select elements from clothing design—leather, beads, tassels, ribbon—are brought together into subtle ornamental arrangements.—Satin fringes, metal—

"W10/5.0" [2]

—Fluo elastic, wood, glass bead, gold coloured beads, metal—

"S11/1.0" [3]

—Glass bead, leather, steel wire—

"W10/1.1" [4]

—Beads, steel wire, fluo elastic—

"W10/9.2" [5]

—Glass bead, pearl, fluo thread, silver—

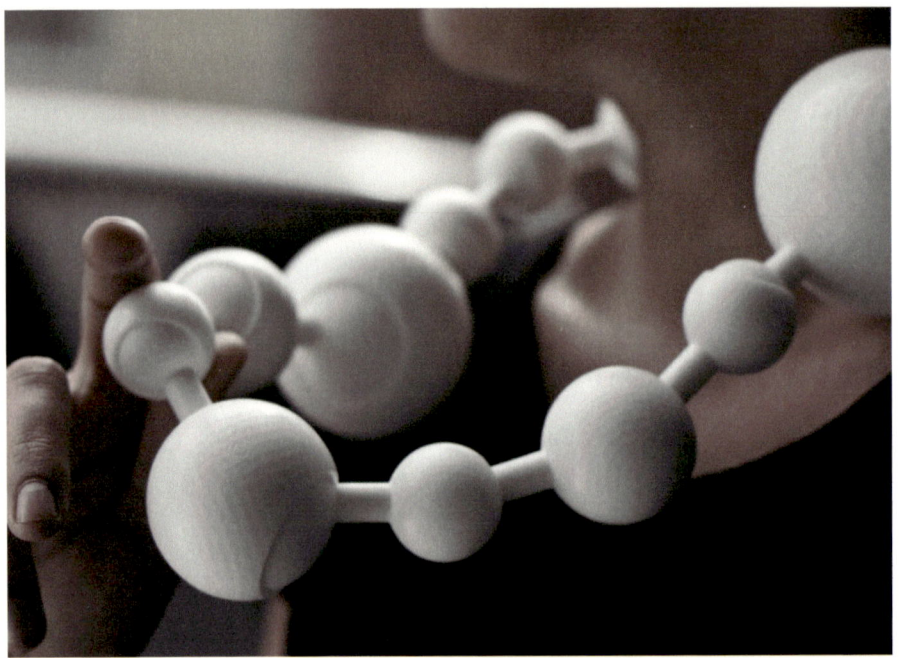

1

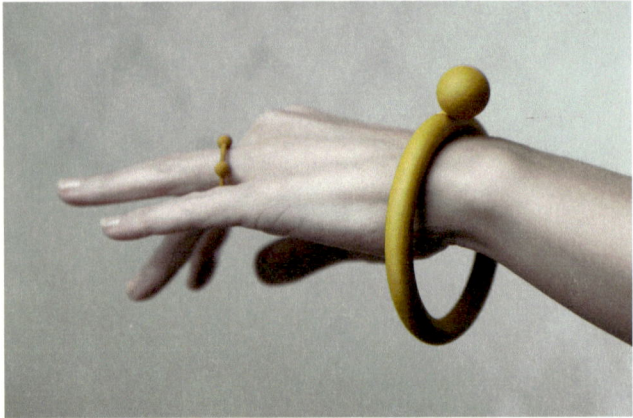

2

BYAMT INC.
"JOINTED JEWELS" [1 & 2]

Jointed Jewels by Alissia Melka-Teichroew began
as an exploration of ball joints and the unification of
disparate elements as a single piece through selective laser sintering. The jewelry collection includes
references to classical jewelry icons, such as Renaissance and Victorian creations, pieces by luxury
brands Bulgari and Cartier, and even human
bone structures.—3D printed polyamide (selective
laser sintering technology)—

"DIAMOND ACRYLIC RING" [3]

byAMT's *Diamond Ring* series playfully subverts
the iconic Tiffany diamond engagement ring,
utilizing a variety of colors, thicknesses and materials.
In addition to acrylic, the rings also come in gold
and silver, and they can be worn individually
or stacked in twos or threes, depending on the width.
—Acrylic—

GITTE NYGAARD
"BUTTON" [1]

In response to Tom Waits' lyric "A diamond that
wants to stay coal," Gitte Nygaard chose to
skip the diamond and stick to the coal for this jewelry
collection built around Binchotan, also known
as white coal. Sourced from oak trees in Japan and
Korea without harming the tree's root structure,
the coal is naturally activated during a controlled
burning process based on a traditional Japanese
method. Unlike common black charcoal, the burning
method for Binchotan consists of capturing the
carbon in the wood without allowing it to escape as
CO_2.—Binchotan certified, sustainable 14 karat
gold from Oro Verde—

SASKIA DIEZ
"BIG ISAR FADE RING" [2]

Inspired by the Isar River that flows by her studio in
Munich, the *Isar* ring series features stones collected
by the artist on the Isar riverbank. Each stone is
cut and polished to yield one unique ring plus a pair of
cufflinks.—Pebble, sterling silver—

2

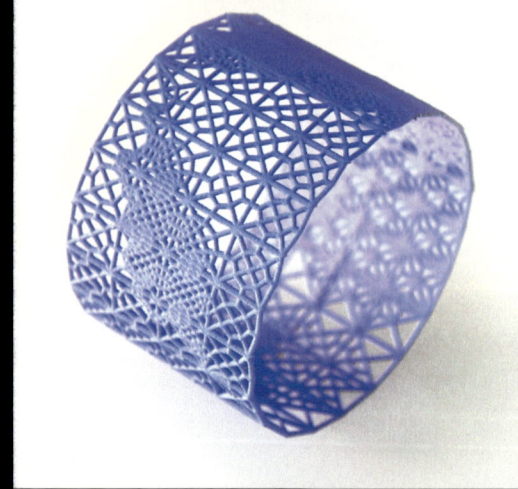

CHRISTINA KARABABA
"MAKING PLEATS_III"

Based on the book *The Fold: Leibniz and the Baroque* by Gilles Deleuze, Christina Karababa's bracelets are sculpted from ABS plastic using the process of fused deposition modeling (FDM). The result is a series of durable yet lightweight fixed forms whose ultrafine layers of crinkles and furrows are deceivingly diaphanous.

—ABS plastic—

MIETTE
"DENTELLE INDIGO"

For their *Dentelle* (French for "lace") cuff, Miette used 3D software to create a lacelike, geometric pattern that was transformed into jewelry using 3D

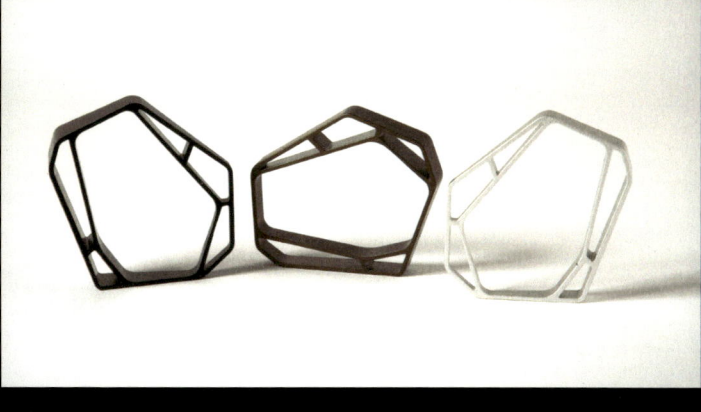

CLAESSON KOIVISTO RUNE
"EVE"

For the *Eve* bracelet by Claesson Koivisto Rune, a single tool is used to produce unique creations through an industrial process. Made from extruded aluminum, a material used often in industry and seldom for jewelry, the bracelet is created by rotating the raw extrusion and simultaneously cutting it at different angles. Further color variations are made by anodizing the surface. This one-size-fits-all bracelet is completely recyclable.—Aluminium—

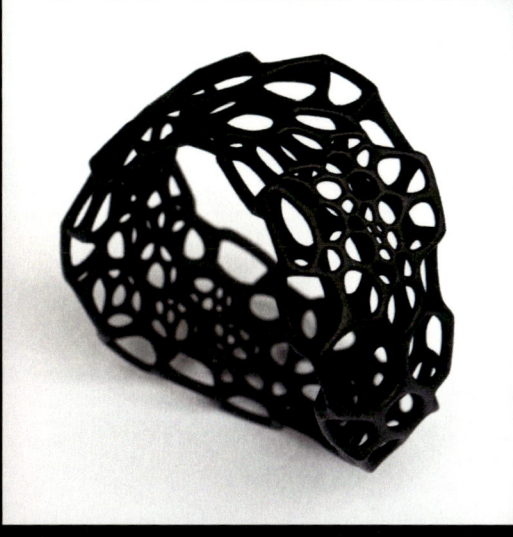

NERVOUS SYSTEM
"SPIRAL CUFF"

Nervous System develops mathematical algorithms and interactive systems to create computer-generated patterns that are reminiscent of natural phenomena, such as cellular structures and rhizome-like networks, which they then translate into jewelry. Designs are 3D laser printed in nylon as the final product, or set in wax to create molds from which to cast metal models, or cut directly onto wool or silicone rubber.
—3D printed stainless steel—

"WAVE BRACELET"
—3D printed nylon—

PURISME
"PURISME BRACELET"

Purisme emancipates carbon from its origins in the world of performance technology to make a range of stylish accessories and jewelry. Made of iridescent black carbon, the *Black Diamond* bracelet is light as a feather, stronger than steel, and (for its makers) aesthetically on par with its carbon counterpart from the world of gemstones.—Carbon—

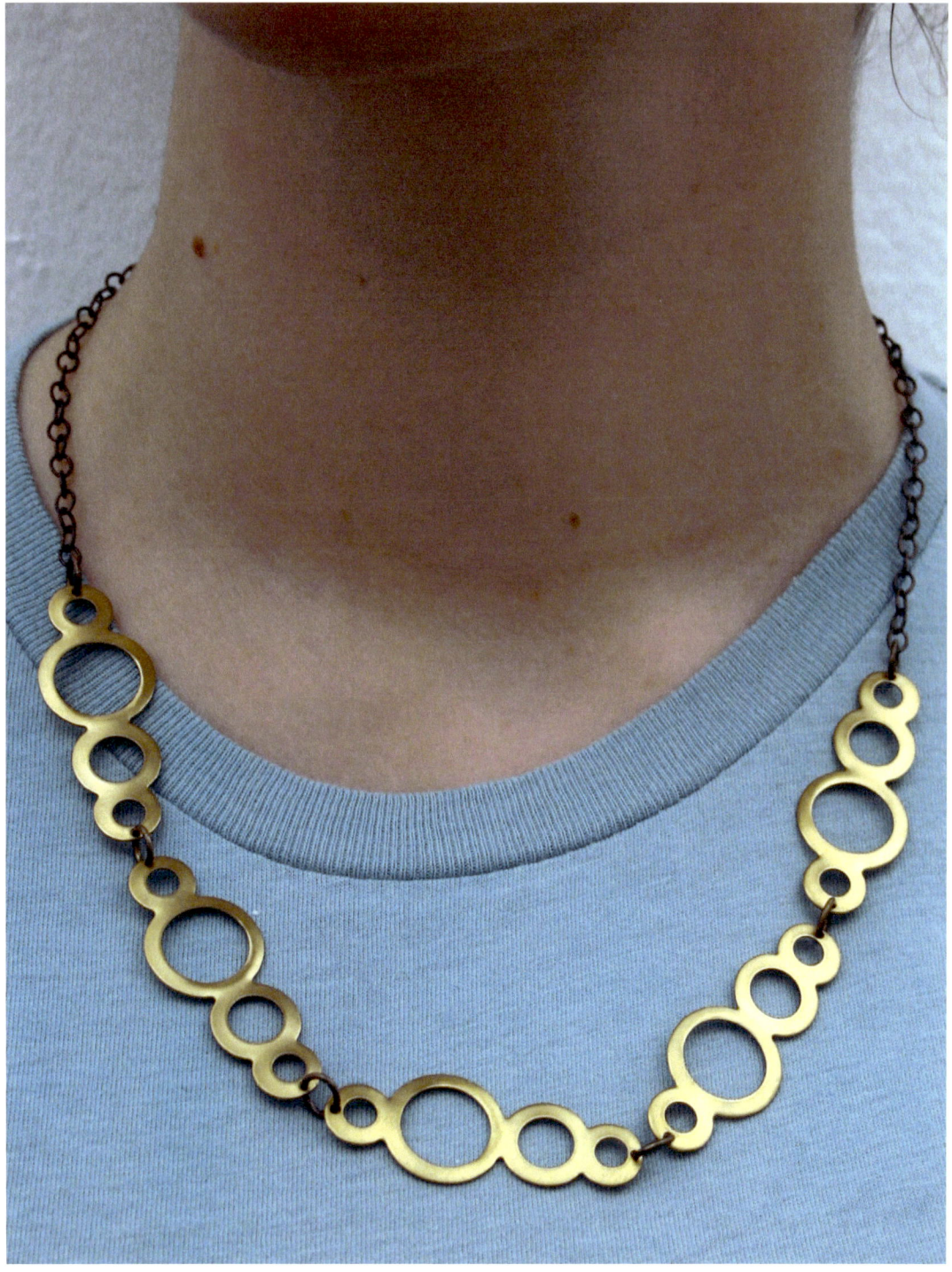

2

LOYALTY & BLOOD
"SQUARE BAR LINK NECKLACE"[1]
"FLAT CIRCLES NECKLACE"[2]
The recent line of brass jewelry pieces by David
Denosowicz and Maggie Doyle of Loyalty &
Blood are studies in the modernist tradition of
geometric design.—Brass—

NUMER6
"KELI. WOOD" [1]

For their limited run series and one-off jewelry pieces, Pamela Martinez & Alejandra Porta of Numer6 reclaim various materials from around the world, from coconut shells and açaí seeds, to vintage glass and wooden beads.—Wooden beads (various sizes), layered wooden bead (5 different types of wood), fabric chain, gold chain, big gold clasp—

"MARYAS. BLACK/ GOLD" [2]

—18 karat gold-plated chain, hand-made glass beads (black and clear glass), metal bead—

2

1

3

2

4

MARION VIDAL
"PICCOLO BALLA NECKLACE" [1]
Drawing inspiration from architectural structures and cloth textures, Marion Vidal—who studied both architecture and fashion—creates bold, sculptural necklaces from colorful ceramic and wooden beads, ribbons, and metal.—Glazed ceramic, golden brass, 100% satin polyester ribbon—

"BONBON NECKLACE" [2]
—Glazed ceramic, golden brass, 100% cotton ribbon—

"NOEUD PAPILLON NECKLACE" [3]
—Glazed ceramic, golden chains, wood pearls—

"LADY TRIANGOLI NECKLACE" [4]
—Glazed ceramic, golden brass, 100% satin polyester ribbon—

1

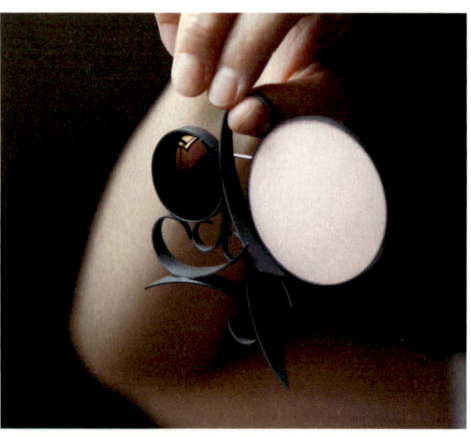

2

JIRO KAMATA
"MOMENTOPIA" [1]

Jiro Kamata's artistry—the repurposing of used camera and sunglasses lenses—sparks meditation on the notions of captured memories, the cool objectivity of the camera, and the gazing into the eye of the beholder. The glass elements, coated with enamel paints or left unadorned, are set into ornamental shapes of blackened silver, and trigger a silent dialogue between the lenses' own characteristics and the wearer's environment.—Painted camera lens, silver—

"ARBORESQUE" [2]
—Painted camera lens, silver—

3

LIAM OF YORK
"MOONLIGHT SONATA
NECKLACE, CLUSTER RING,
ARROWS RING,
BRAID RINGS, METEOR
SHOWER BRACELET,
COBRA BRACELET" [3]

In the sculptural jewelry of Rebecca Wolsten,
geometric forms hearken back to ancient and natural
imagery: gold triangles refer to arrows found in
pyramids, silver link bracelets are derived from
a cobra's sinuous form, and ball chain necklaces recall
meteor showers, or the shape of a comet's trail.—

SASKIA DIEZ
"GOLD BIG KNOT NECKLACE"
The delicate sterling silver chains of the *BIG KNOT* necklace by Saskia Diez are twice tied, reminiscent of traditional Chinese knotting. The knots also conceal an adjustment mechanism that can be used to vary the length of the chains.—14 karat gold—

1

2

3

SABRINA DEHOFF
"HOPE & FEAR STATEMENT CHOKER COLLIER" [1]

The gold-plated collier by Sabrina Dehoff offers a simple yet elegant intervention to add instant glam to nearly any outfit. The long binding allows the wearer to chose how tightly around the neck it is worn.—Leather, 23 karat gold-plated—

WILLEMIJN DE GREEF
"ZUIDERZEEWERKEN II, HALSSIERAAD GEVLOCHTEN TOUW" [2]

Willemijn de Greef's creations recall nautical and aquatic imagery, inspired by her upbringing in Zeeland, a coastal province and network of islands in the southern Netherlands. In her work, fisherman's ropes in hemp and cotton and boat chains are transformed into necklaces, while elements from traditional clothing from the region are enlarged and reinterpreted into brooches and necklaces.—Hemp rope, silver—

"ZUIDERZEEWERKEN II, HALSSIERAAD LEGUAAN" [3]
—Hemp rope, linnen thread, silver—

MIKE HOLMES
"TOY PENDANT" [2]

Evoking images of decorative tribal bangles or even a child's rattle, the smoothly sculptured *Toy Pendant* by Mike Holmes in recycled wood and bone is designed to be worn in any direction; there is no "up" or "down."—Walnut, bone, recycled hardwood, sterling silver—

2

3

STUDY O PORTABLE
"FLOOR NECKLACE" [1]

Study O Portable deconstructs the floor for their aptly named *Floor Necklace:* here, a piece of miniature and checkered flooring made of linoleum and vintage oak falls apart to reveal a cascading necklace.—Linoleum, vintage oak—

"BAUM" [3]

Inspired by the traditional German Baumkuchen (a layered cake), the *Baum* bracelets by Study O Portable are created by layering colored ceramic resin onto a rotating spit. The resulting tree-like trunk is sliced and polished into individual bracelets of varying thickness that—like a tree trunk's cross-sections—expose the intricate pattern of growth that develops during the creative process.—Ceramic resin—

MIKE HOLMES
"ANTI-WAR MEDAL 2" [1]
The *Anti-War Medal 2* by Mike Holmes was created
in reaction to the war in Iraq and makes a clear
statement about the U.S. involvement in it: a wooden
pentagon is pierced by bone bombs surrounded by
red enamel blood.—Walnut, bone, enameled wood—

"HERE I AM" [2]
The glittering sculptural piece crafted of mirror, wood
and brass by Mike Holmes evokes images of a
precious tortoise in a mystical forest, or crystalline
forms growing out of an otherworldly shell or
stone. Adorning the body or clothing, it draws atten-
tion not only to itself but also the wearer as its
tiled surface reflects the immediate surroundings.
—Recycled walnut, mirror, brass—

1

2

3

KARIN SEUFERT
"NIKELACE" [3]

In her recent work realized in the *Modern Fetishes* collection, Karin Seufert addresses the notion of the icon. Well-known logotypes from popular brands such as Nike or Puma are appropriated, manipulated, and transformed into jewelry, raising questions like: Who owns whom? Is it the jewelry itself, or the original brand that sells?—PVC, artificial leather, elastic—

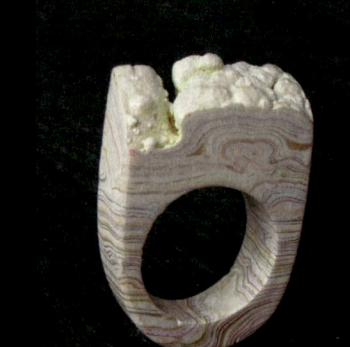

ADI ZAFFRAN
WEISLER
"BULLET RING"

Once separated from its original function, the bullet becomes an aesthetic object. No two of Adi Zaffran's *Bullet Rings* will ever be the same: the form of each bullet is randomly determined by its trajectory and its contact with surfaces along its path. Every bullet retains the traces, or memories, of its journey, from the moment it was fired until it was picked up.––Spare bullet (brass, copper, lead), copper ring––

HAFSTEINN JULIUSSON
"GROWING JEWELRY"

Hafsteinn Juliusson's *Growing Jewelry* collection is a synthesis of glamour and gardening. Each sterling silver piece comes planted with Icelandic moss and the expectation that its wearer will tend to it with care. If properly maintained, the moss can stay green for 8 to 12 months.—Sterling silver, Icelandic moss—

NAOKO OGAWA
"ALONG WITH YOU"

The partner rings of the project *Along with you* by Naoko Ogawa feature a discrete golden notch formed when the rings overlap. Following the curve of your partner's finger, the ring is a constant reminder of the other's presence.—18 karat white gold, 18 karat yellow gold—

SILVA/ BRADSHAW
"SHIFT"

The multidisciplinary design team founded by Matthew Bradshaw and Sergio Silva makes conceptually driven objects that play with principles of geometry and the relationships between forms. Their *Sfero* ring, for example, consists of a gold vermeil sphere cut with three differently sized ring holes, leaving the remaining negative spaces to be filled by the wearer's finger.—Rose gold vermeil—

GIORGIO VIGNA
"FILO"

Giorgio Vigna works in a variety of materials, from hand-blown Murano glass to copper, magnets, and synthetic mesh. His creations push the boundaries between jewelry and sculpture, examining the interaction of form and function, nature and fantasy. Simple yet intricate, his *Filo* ring is just that: a mass of gold yarn balled up into a ring.—Yellow gold—

2

3

EVERT NIJLAND
"NECKLACE VENEZIA"[2]
See description on p 47—Glass, electric wire, gold—

BELMACZ
"BROWN ASSORTED BABYLOVES"[1]
Traditional gemcraft meets contemporary luxury in the creations by Julia Muggenburg, the designer behind Belmacz. Her one-off, limited edition adornments feature powerful and poetic combinations: earthy or rare materials such as ebony, amber, fossilized bone, pearls, or coral are merged with fine metal accents.
—Banded agate, moss agate, oxidized silver—

"AUGUSTUS BROOCH"[3]
—Tahitian pearl, chrysoprase, pink opal, antique amber, hawk's eye, 18 karat yellow gold—

1

YOKO IZAWA
"BLOSSOM" [1]

A sense of ambiguity or transience
is what designer Yoko Izawa
aims to convey with her "veiled"
jewelry. The artist creates finely
knitted enclosures from elastic
nylon yarn, which she then adorns
with lightweight polypropylene,
acrylic, pearls, or metal. The result
is a compelling jewelry collection
that is organic in form, and one
that displays harmonious colors.—
Lycra/nylon, polypropylene—

"PETAL" [2]

—Lycra/nylon, polypropylene,
silver—

2

NERVOUS SYSTEM
"LARGE CORAL BROOCH" [3]

Nervous System develops mathematical algorithms
and interactive systems to create computer-generated
patterns that are reminiscent of natural phenomena, such as cellular structures and rhizome-like
networks, which they then translate into jewelry.
Designs are 3D laser printed in nylon as the
final product, or set in wax to create molds from which
to cast metal models, or cut directly onto wool or
silicone rubber.—Stainless steel—

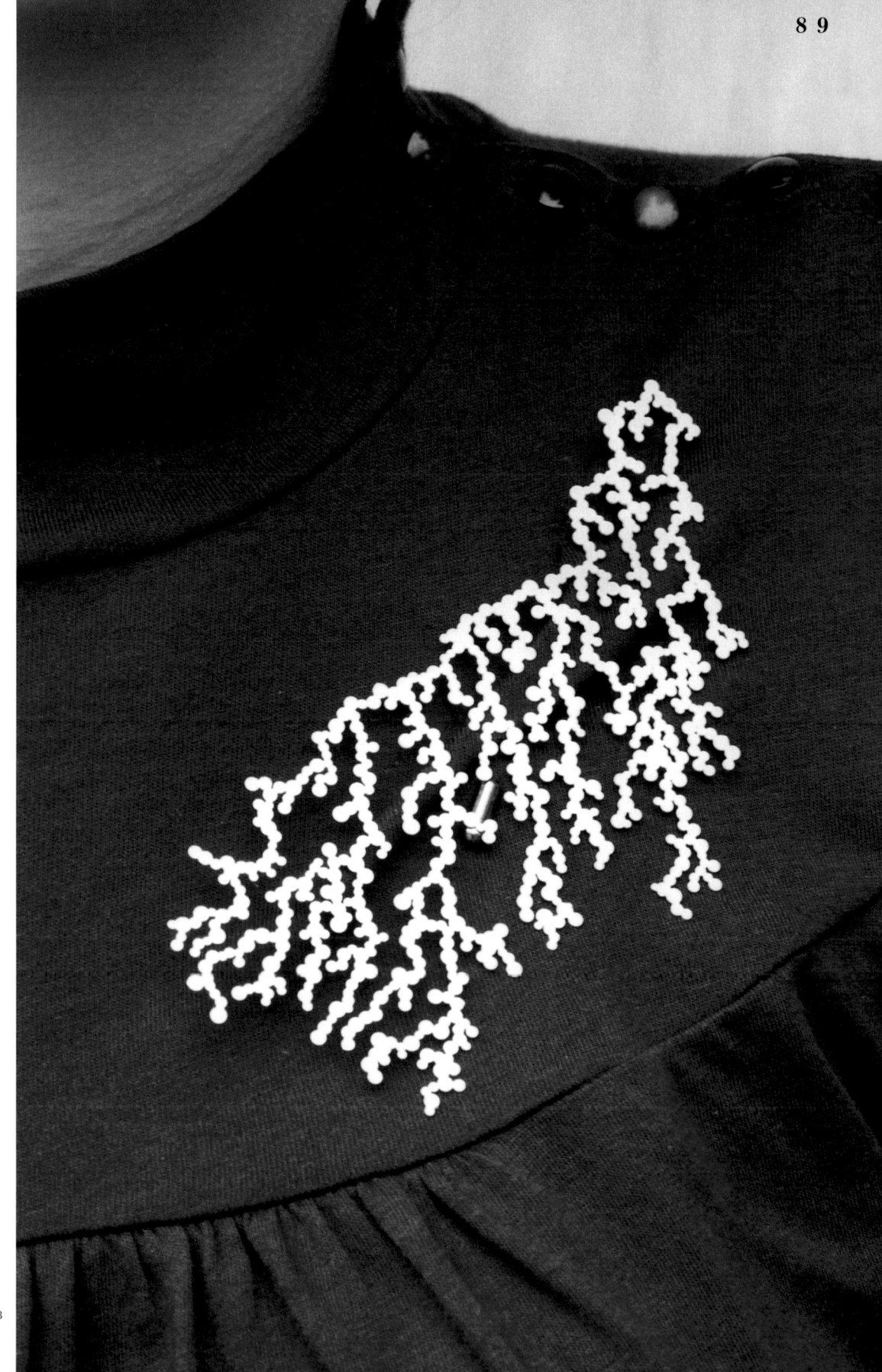

LAD
~ CONCEPT

Y G

PIA ALEBORG
"APARTFROM"
In this series of subtle and wearable inventions, Pia
Aleborg removes elements of everyday life—such as
electric cords and forgotten socks—from their context
and transforms them into jewelry.—1: Yellow rubber,
sock, gold-plated metal chain—2: Electric Cord,
gold-plated metal chain—

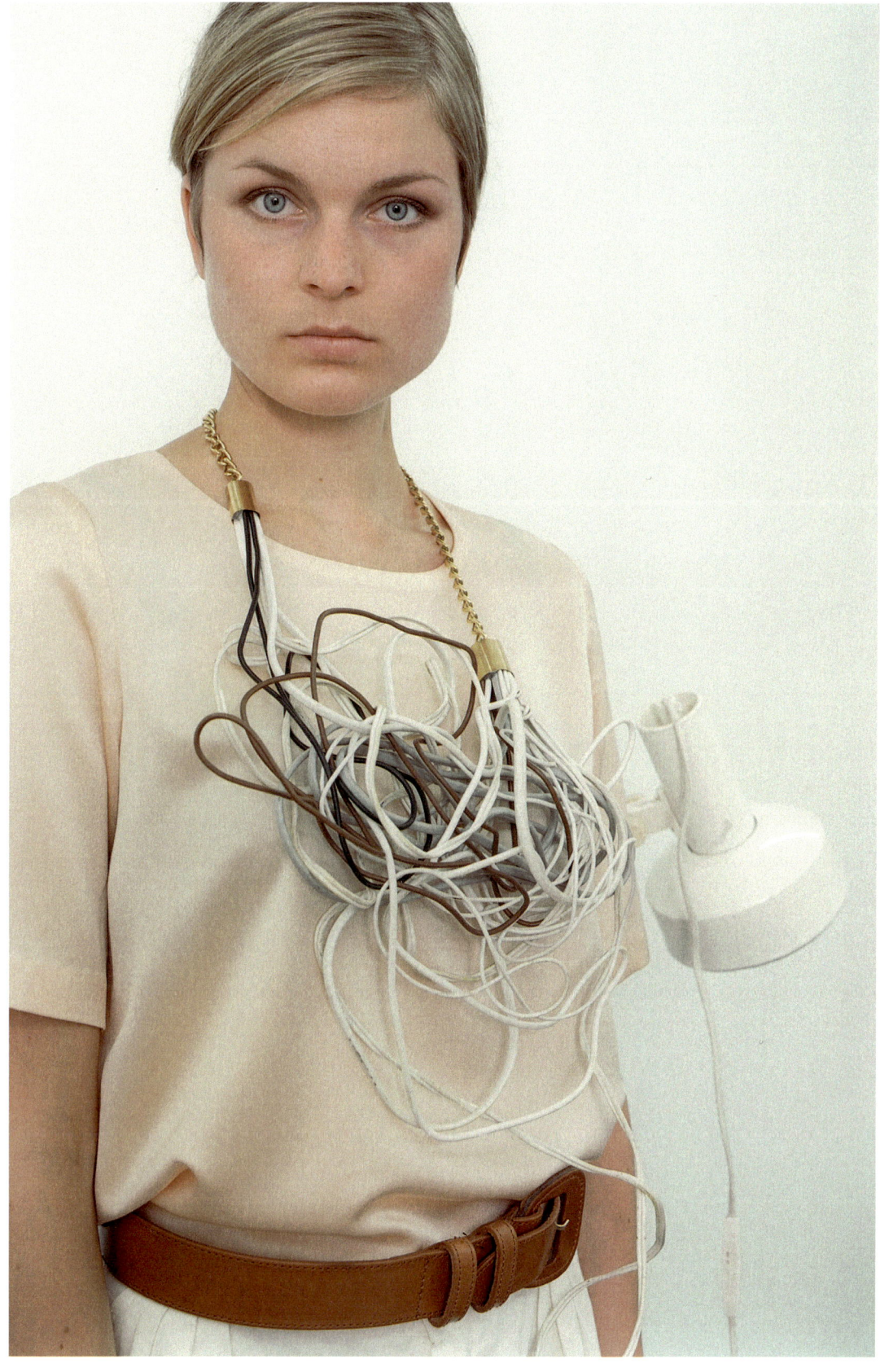

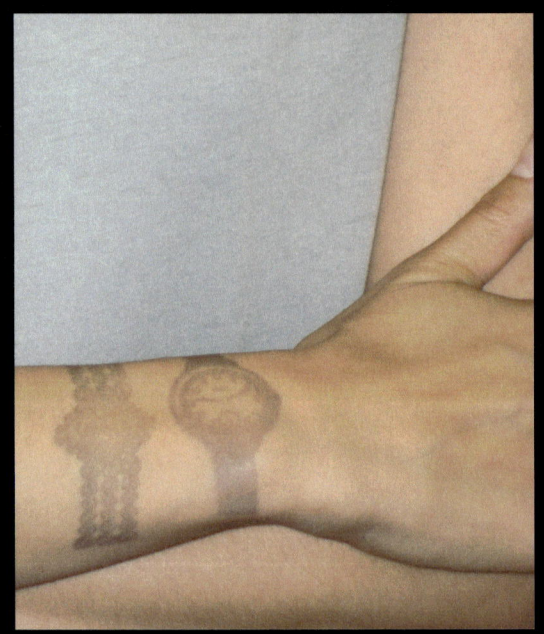

AZUMI AND DAVID
(A ' N ' D)
"EXTRAORDINARY"
Is the reproduction of a piece of jewelry still a piece

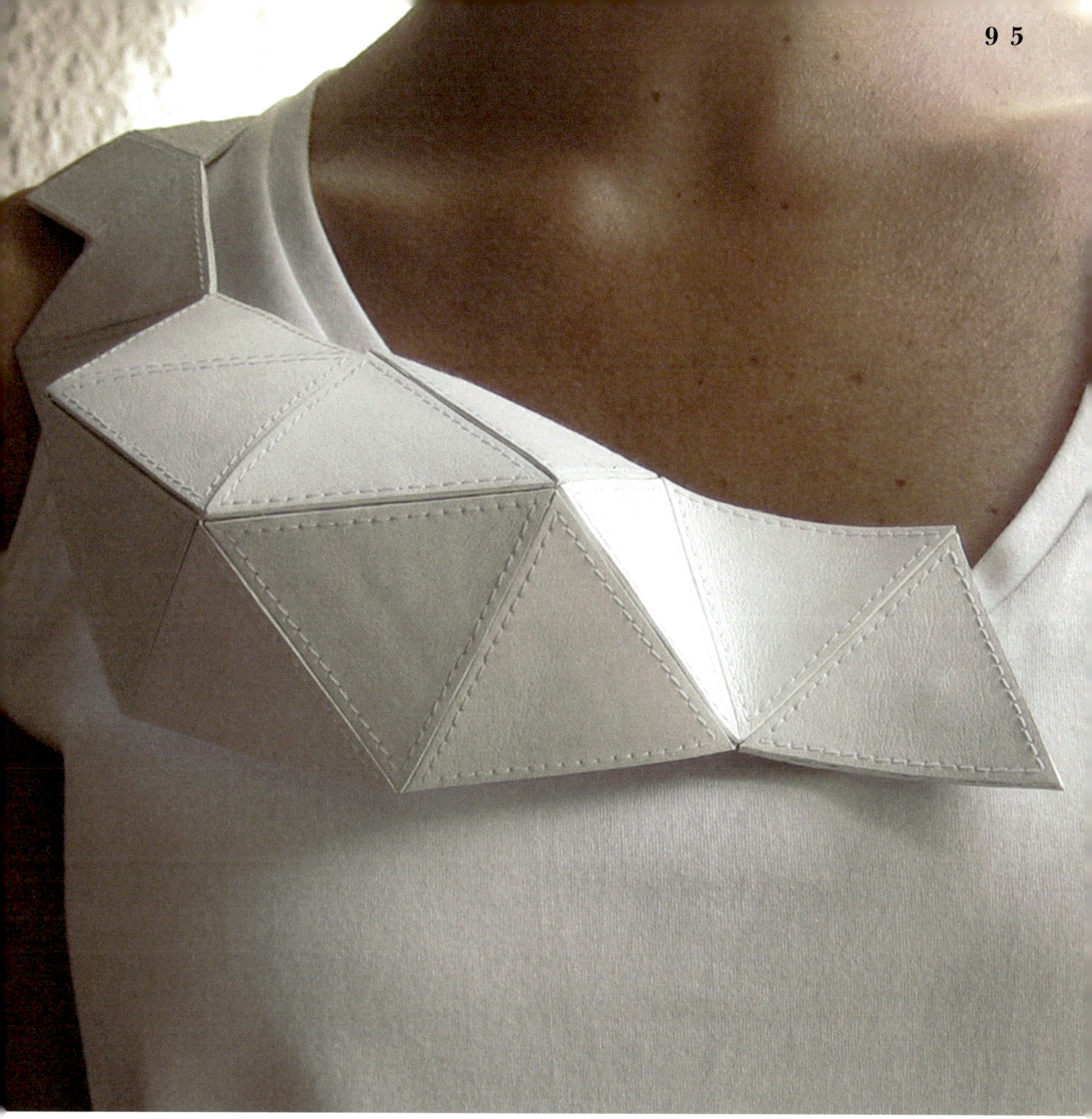

1

2

ANTIATOMS
"BIG LEATHER BROOCH" [1]
Each piece in this collection by ANTIATOMS is a puzzle, one that can be solved by studying the material used, the cutting pattern, and the assembly of the parts. The leather accessories emphasize volume thanks to the weight of the material and the deconstruction of the cutting pattern. The basic color palette of the collection was chosen to signal both the moment of clarity when a puzzle has been solved (white), or the elements that hinder its solution (black).—White/black leather—

"LEATHER NECKLACE" [2]
—White leather—

V I J 5
"S A M P L E S E R I E S"

The Newspaper Wood jewelry collection by design
group Vij5 may be likened to wearable archives.
The patented Newspaper Wood consists of layers of
newspaper pressed into logs that are then further
treated like real wood. When cut, the newspaper
layers resemble wood grain. For the *Newspaper Wood
Sample Series,* the news of a single day was contained
in a pendant. The date of the used newspaper is
engraved into the brass setting.—Newspaper Wood,
brass, doublé necklace—

Ø30.25.01.11

Ø40.25.01.11

Ø110.25.01.11

1

BEATRICE BROVIA
"THE UNAVOIDABLENESS OF
EDUCATION, NECKLACE" [1]
In her unique conceptual creations, Beatrice Brovia
considers jewelry a language with symbolic
value. Important as ritualized objects, the artist also
sees jewelry as capable of identifying and marking
a body.—Natural resin, flax silk, latex hose—

"ANTROPOGENESIS,
NECKLACES" [2]
—Foam, textile, silver, latex hose—

ANDREA AUER
"KULTURPERLEN"[1]
PVC-, Bakelite-, and polyester-
coated metal beads—more
commonly occurring as drapery
weights—are just three of the
many unconventional materials
used by Andrea Auer for her
jewelry creations. Her collection
of matching PVC earrings,
collier, and muff, or her Bakelite
bracelets and chains, are as at
home in couture fashion as they
are in prêt-a-porter, blurring
the boundaries between art and
ornamentation.—Polyesterfabric
metal—

"THE WHITE TUBE"[2]
—Cable (PVC)—

HANNA HEDMAN
"WHAT YOU TELL
IS NOT ALWAYS WHAT YOU
EXPERIENCED"

In this collection of sculptural jewelry, Hanna Hedman
explores the spaces between reality and fantasy,
beauty and pain, fragility and resilience. Thin layers
of oxidized silver and copper sheets are combined with
silver, paint, textile and synthetic fibers to create symbolic representations of the human condition.—Silver,
oxidized silver, copper, paint, textile, synthetic fibers—

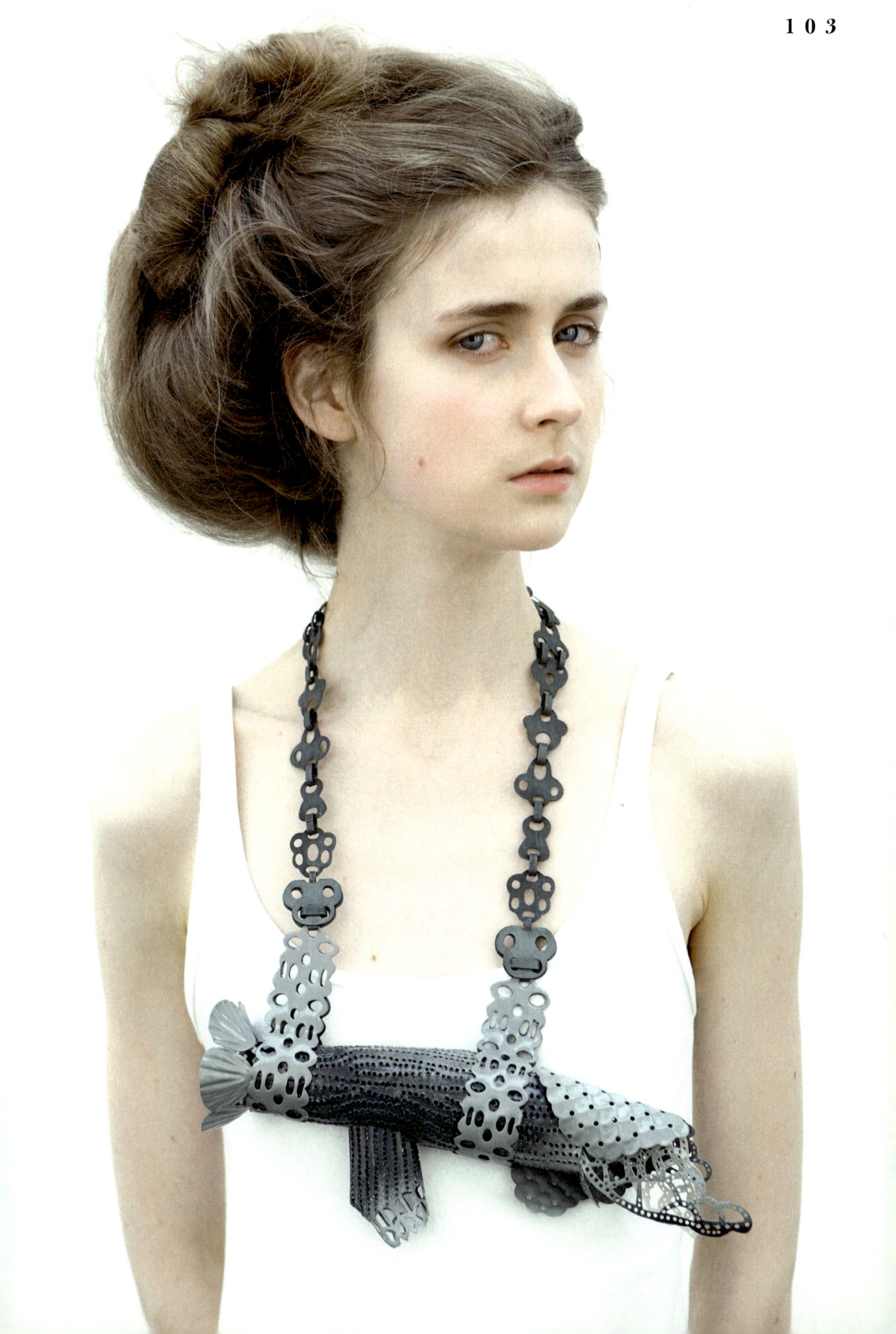

2

KIM BUCK

"GOLD, JEWELLERY, GOLD,
JEWELLERY, GOLD....." [1]

Kim Buck fashions wearable pieces that offer reflections on the form, meaning, and material
of jewelry. His pieces, often made of gold, silver, and
even metallic foil, reference conventional design
concepts while simultaneously deconstructing the
same conventions.—Gold—

"PREPARATIONS, #38-583A-C" [2]

—Ring, acrylic—

1

2

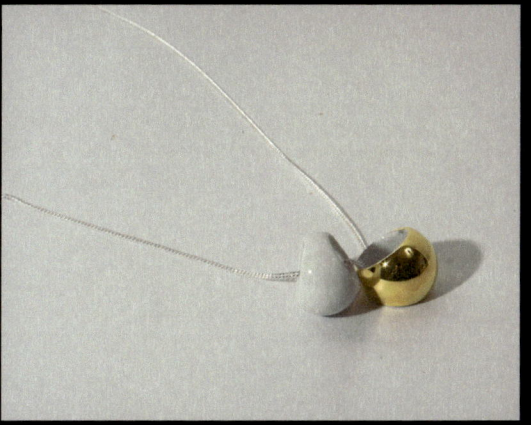

3

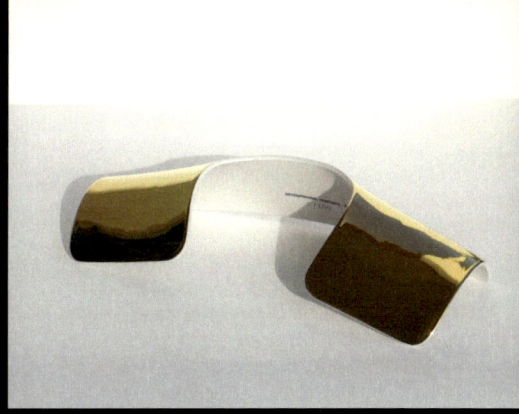

4

UNCOMMON MATTERS
"SHOULDERPIECE" [1 & 4]

The AU[79] series by Amelie Riech for Uncommon
Matters turns traditional porcelain craftwork
on its head and blurs the lines between fashion and
jewelry. Delicately curved collars, cuffs and
pendants are glazed, or hand-painted with gold or
platinum, or refined with silver chain. The
pieces are handcrafted by commission by the traditional German porcelain manufacturers.—Gilded
porcelain—

"BRACELET" [2]
—Porcelain, platinum—

"RINGCHAIN" [3]
— Gilded porcelain, 925 silver chain—

1

BLESS
"N°42 PLÄDOYER DER JETZTZEIT, JEWELED EATING IRONS 2" [1]

Blurring the line between accessory and jewelry, the *Servering* piece by Bless functions as its name describes: as a serving container as well as a ring.—silver—

"N°26 CABLE JEWELLERY" [2]

The *Cable Jewellery* collection by Bless takes the connectors of everyday—electronic objects—and elevates them to the level of jewelry. Cables, usually more of a nuisance and kept out of sight, are transformed, using additional elements such as feathers, fur, crystals, pearls, and wooden beads, into objects of beauty and ornamentation. Clients may have their own cables turned into "cable jewelry" by ordering from a range of predefined styles.—Material mix—

IVY

~GOTHIC

1

O S
"CLUSTER OF BONES" [1]
Inspired by tribal jewelry discovered during exoctic
travels, Paul Jatayna, Kat Medina, and AJ Oman-
dac of OS Accessories began making realistic animal
bone replicas from polyurethane cast molds. Combining these replicas with industrial elements such
as screws, bolts, and chains lend their handcrafted
pieces a contemporary feel.—Polyurethane, rhodium-
plated brass chain, lobster clasp—

"RIBCAGE" [2]
—Polyurethane, metal, rhodium-plated brass chain,
lobster clasp—

1

ENFANTS PERDUS
"GREAT HERON SKULL RING, HEAVY PUERARIA RING, AND ELEGANT PUERARIA RING" [1]

Enfants Perdus creates an aesthetic inspired by art
deco and also gothic romanticism with their ornate
floral detailing, weathered metals, and precious
gemstones, such as pale white sapphires, diamonds,
ink black onyx and pearls. Sterling silver interwoven
with gold is hand-treated with antiquing washes so
that a rich patina develops over the course of
human wear.—Diamond, black pearl, sterling silver,
18 karat yellow gold—

"ORCHIDACEAE
CRYSTAL DAGGER PENDANT
(VARIOUS STONES)" [2]
—Diamond pale white sapphire, ink black onyx,
smoke and milk quartz, sterling silver, 18 karat white
gold, 18 karat yellow gold—

"ORCHIDACEAE CROSS
NECKLACE" [3]
—Chain: 18"; Pendant: 1–1/4" x 2". Gothic cross,
sterling silver chain links—

"HEAVY WHITE ORCHIDACEAE
CURB BRACELET" [4]
—Pale white sapphires, sterling silver, 18 karat
white gold—

LILLOT
"GENE BRACELET"

Liliam Higa puts a contemporary spin on tribal
jewelry, inspired by her studies of traditional crafts
in Okinawa, along with her upbringing and studies
in São Paulo. Beads, seeds, coconut, and crystals
count among the materials she combines with gold-
plated brass, bronze, and reclaimed silver into her
creations.—Reclaimed silver, black agate, fresh water
pearls, brass, polyester—

2

PATRIK MUFF
"MEDALLION" [1]
—Medallion: sterling silver, black synthetic inlay—

PATRIK MUFF
BY NYMPHENBURG
"ESSENTIALS" [2]
Porcelain factory Nymphenburg collaborated with
jewelry designer Patrik Muff to create a line of jewelry
based on iconic symbols in handmade glazed porcelain
embellished with filigree gold and silver as well as
precious gems. The *Essentials* collection depicts
symbols reflecting the human condition, such as the
skull for impermanence, the anchor for hope, and
the heart for love.—Porcelain pendants; Anchor
chains: sterling silver—

1

PATRIK MUFF
"LETZTER AUSWEG LUXUS" [1]
See description on p. 10—Skull rings: pavé,
yellow and white gold 750|000, brown and white
diamonds, pink sapphires—

"GOLD" [2]
—*Carlotta* and *Eternity* stone rings: red, yellow,
and white gold 750|000; diamonds, sapphire,
tourmaline, kunzite; Beetle ring: red gold 750|000;
approx. 1.5 carats of pavé, white and violet
diamonds; Skull ring: white gold 750|000, 1.8 carats
of brown diamonds; Pendant and anchor chains:
yellow gold 750|000, various motifs; *Les fleurs du
mal* anchor bracelet: yellow gold 750|000—

BLACK SHEEP & PRODIGAL SONS

"LOVERS SCRIMSHAW NECKLACE"

The word "scrimshaw" is derived from a North American slang expression referring to the decoration of shells or bone by a loafing seafarer. With this collection for his jewelry label Black Sheep & Prodigal Sons, Derrick R. Cruz seeks to preserve this American tradition by using precious metals and fossilized Alaskan mammoth tusk as his canvases. Each piece is engraved with hundreds of minuscule lines to bestow a contemporary yet timeless aesthetic.— Fossilized alaskan woolly mammoth ivory, oxidized sterling silver, 18 karat rose gold—

JOOMI LIM
"METAL-LUXE" [1]
Design duo Joomi Lim and Xavier Ricolfi present an upscale take on punk rock
and tribal motifs. Edgy elements such as spikes, studs, or chunky chain
are reworked in precious metals and playfully combined with pearls, crystals,
and fringe. —Swarovski crystal/brass chain dipped in rose gold/spikes
dipped in rhodium—

"SAVE THE QUEEN" [2]
—Swarovski crystal and pearls/brass chain, brass spikes dipped in antique
rhodium—

DEMITASSE
JEWELRY
"DEMITASSE CLASSIC
COLLECTION"

Demitasse Jewelry takes its inspiration from the
tradition of lavish tableware collections of days
past. Opulent spoons and miniature knives in gold,
decorated with diamonds and sapphires, incorporate historical references in their design. Made to
be worn around the neck, the creations blend the
notions of heirloom tableware with heirloom jewelry.
—Mixed metals, sterling silver, 14 karat rose
and yellow gold, diamonds—

DIGBY & IONA
"DIAMOND SIGNET RING"

The sterling silver *Diamond Signet Ring* by Digby &
Iona doubles as a working wax seal that leaves
an imprint of a diamond when used. The words "None
Cuttes a Diamond But a Diamond" along the
ring's edge quotes John Marston's satirical play from
1604, *The Malcontent,* adding a witty philosophical edge. The series also includes diamond-shaped
pendants and cufflinks.—Sterling silver—

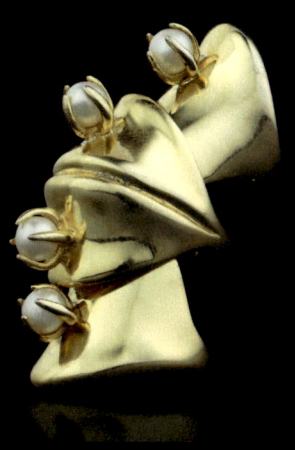

BIJULES
"DETACHED ARTICULATED
RING IN 3 PARTS"
See description on p. 37—14 karat gold, white pearl—

ENFANTS
PERDUS
"ORCHIDACEAE
SKULL CLUTCH PIN
BROOCHES"
See description on p. 114—Diamond,
pale white sapphires, sterling
silver, 18 karat yellow gold, 18 karat
white gold—

HANNAH
MARTIN
"IMPERIAL EAGLE
TINY TALISMAN"
See description on p. 40—18 carat
yellow gold—

ELIZABETH
KNIGHT
"FLAT TOP RING"
See description on p. 220—Brass—

1

2

3

AOI KOTSUHIROI
"FLOATING SHADOWS" [1]

Aoi Kotsuhiroi's *Body Objects,* a series of one-off
wearable sculptures, are a dream-like synthesis
of poetry and erotic brutality. Pieces are woven together
from eclectic materials such as Urushi lacquered
horn, antique beads, leather, fabric, human hair,
embroidered silk thread, and pit-fired porcelain skulls.
The artist defines herself not as a jewelry maker
but as a novelist: each of her collections is accompanied by poetic titles, and the series within the
collections are described as chapters.—Crocodile
leather (partly lacquered), bison leather, horse
hair, Urushi lacquered horn, antique Roman 24 karat
gold beads (circa 100–400 AD)—

"DAY DREAM" [2]
—Pit-fired porcelain (skulls), human hair, Japanese
antique indigo fabric, silk thread, antique Roman black
glass beads (circa 100–400 AD), Urushi lacquer—

"ENDLESS" [3]
—Urushi lacquered horns, horse hair, linen thread,
bison leather (partly lacquered)—

"NAKED SOLITUDE" [4]
—Antique buddhist carnelian prayer beads,
embroidered silk thread, leather, human hair, Urushi
lacquer—

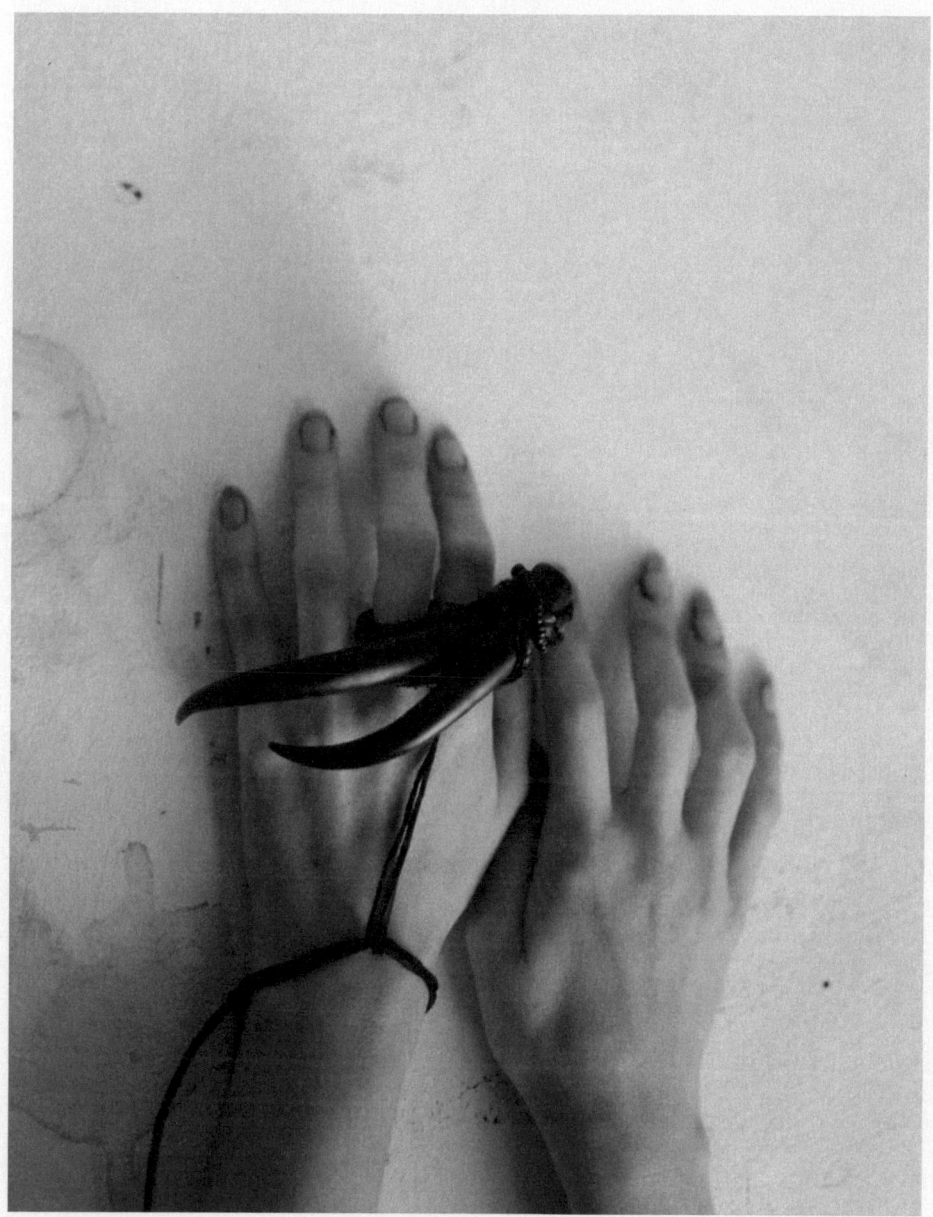

2

AOI KOTSUHIROI
"SLEEPING SHADOW" [1]
—Urushi lacquered horns, horse hair, bison leather,
Urushi lacquer—

"ALL SORTS OF RAINS" [2]
—Urushi lacquered horn, horse hair, silk thread,
antique Roman 24 karat gold beads (circa 100–400 AD),
pi-fired porcelain (skull beads), leather—

MARIA FRANCISCA PEPE
"OSIRIS NECKLACE"

The *Veleno* collection by Maria Francisca Pepe takes as its inspiration the sinuous sensuality and mystique of the serpent. For the *Isis* necklace and *Osiris* bracelet, silk rope is wrapped in gold chains and charms—a tribal declination of the design label's signature "tubular" necklace.—Ruthenium-plated brass chains, Vergolino rope, gold-plated brass, metal, pearl, turquoises.—

EVERT NIJLAND
NECKLACE 'FRA ANGELICO'
FROM THE
FRAGMENTS SERIES
See description on p. 47—Handwoven linen, silk,
antique gold thread, silver—

ROARKE NEW YORK
"COLLAR AND GLOVES"
The collar and gloves by Roarke New York are a
discreet intervention by the world of jewelry
into fashion. The hand-beaded satin collar adds gentle
sophistication to T-shirts, while the mesh demi
gloves adorned with sequins and glass beads contrast
with rock and roll glam.—Collar: Satin, pearls,
Gloves: mesh, sequins, glass beads—

1

KARIN SEUFERT
"NO TITLE" [1]
See description on p. 83—PVC, press-button—

LILLOT
"KAMI NECKLACE" [2]
Liliam Higa puts a contemporary spin on tribal
jewelry, inspired by her studies of traditional
crafts in Okinawa, along with her upbringing and
studies in São Paulo. Beads, seeds, coconut, and
crystals count among the materials she combines
with gold-plated brass, bronze, and reclaimed
silver into her creations.—Rayon fringe, vintage
brass chain—

2

1

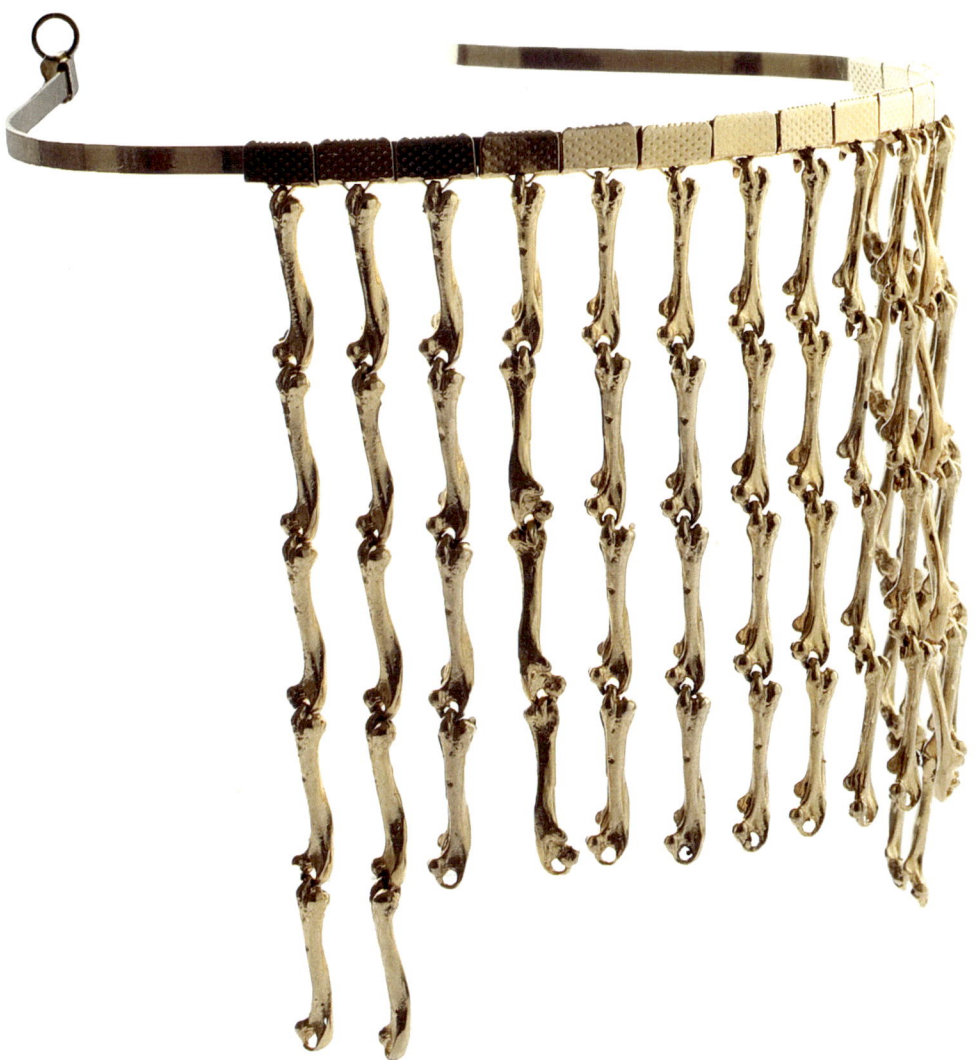

3

A L Y S O N   F O X
"O B J E C T   1"[1] & "O B J E C T   4"[2]
See description on p. 33—Cast bronze—

B I J U L E S
"B O N E C R U S H E R   F A C E   V E I L"[3]
See description on p. 37—14 karat gold tiara,
click/lock bone links—

1

2

3

RP/ENCORE
"NECKLACES FROM PARK COLLECTION" [1]

The creations by Reid Peppard of RP/Encore raise associations with folkloric imagery and spark debate on what we wear, why we wear them and where they come from. The designer uses traditional and modern methods of taxidermy as well as metal casts of animal teeth, bones, and organs to transform animals normally considered repulsive into wearable objects of wonder.—A selection of sterling silver, and gold plated sterling silver jewelry, in addition to one sterling silver plated brass necklace with a leather strap.—

"DOUBLE RAT HEADDRESS" [2]
—Two large taxidermy rats with 100 Swarovski Crystal elements hand applied to each tail (200 in total) with garnet and peridot eyes, small metal skull all built onto black velvet band.—

"LONDON CAUGHT MOUSE BROOCH" [3]
—Taxidermy mouse rear on black leather and 22 karat gold-plated brooch backing.—

"LARGE WHITE RAT BRACELET" [4]
—Large white rat preserved using traditional taxidermy methods, with garnet eyes, and solid sterling silver chain and clasp.—

4

TITHI KUTCHAMUCH
"COMPANION PARROT"
See description on p. 144—Bronze, silver, aluminum—

TITHI KUTCHAMUCH
"COMPANION PARROT" [1]

Man's best friends have been designed to go wherever
their owner wears them in this jewelry series by
Tithi Kutchamutch. Pieces range from silver rings and
bracelets that feature semi-detached sculpted
animals in zebrano wood, bronze, and silver, to pieces
where the animals are integrated into the shape,
such as circles of pigs, or rabbits in aluminum, that
serve as bracelets and rings.—Bronze,
silver, aluminum—

"SECRET FRIEND
FAMILY" [2]

—Brunt oak, zebrano, bronze, silver 925, aluminum—

CYN
~POP

D I

1

2

DENISE JULIA REYTAN
"LIVING MEMORY"

With her *Living Memory* collection, Denise Julia
Reytan continues her hallmark approach of combining
diverse elements. While the designer has long
worked with plastic and silicone, this series focuses
on cut gemstones. The poetic compositions play
with the tension arising from the juxtaposition of the
artificial with the natural, and the individuality
of the diverse components.

—1: Variscite, rose quartz, red agate, smoky quartz,
coral, betel nuts, plastic, reconstr. turquoise—

—2: Anden opal, smoky quartz, chalcedon, carnelian,
greenish smoky quartz, silver, plastic—

—3: Smoky quartz, heterosit, reconstructed coral,
onyx, silver, plastic, cable—

2

3

4

DENISE JULIA REYTAN
"LIVING MEMORY"
—1: Smoky quartz, turquoise, silver, plastic, steel—

—2: Reconstructed coral, reconstructed turquoise, smoky quartz, silver—

—3: Reconstructed coral, reconstructed turquoise, smoky quartz, white agate, silver, acrylic glass—

—4: Lavender quartz, amethyst, white agate, acrylic glass, silver, plastic—

B R E V I T Y

"O C E A N" [1]

"M O U N T A I N" [2]

"A R R O W" [3]

"B I R D S" [4]

"H O R S E S H O E" [5]

Inspired by Native American symbols, Brevity Design celebrates in its *Lines* collection the simple elegance of a basic geometric element. Employing a reduced color palette that echoes Native American themes, acrylic pictograms are attached to silver chains, with each element connected to its own chain.—Acrylic pendant, sterling silver chain—

1

2

3

4

5

1

ALEXANDRA BLAK
"YASMIN EARRING" [1]
"MADAME NEON CHOKER" [2]
The hand-sculpted creations by designer Alexandra
Anson for her jewelry label Alexandra Blak are
characterized by minimalist, futuristic forms and
materials, focusing on Lucite, silver, textiles,
and stone.—Lucite—

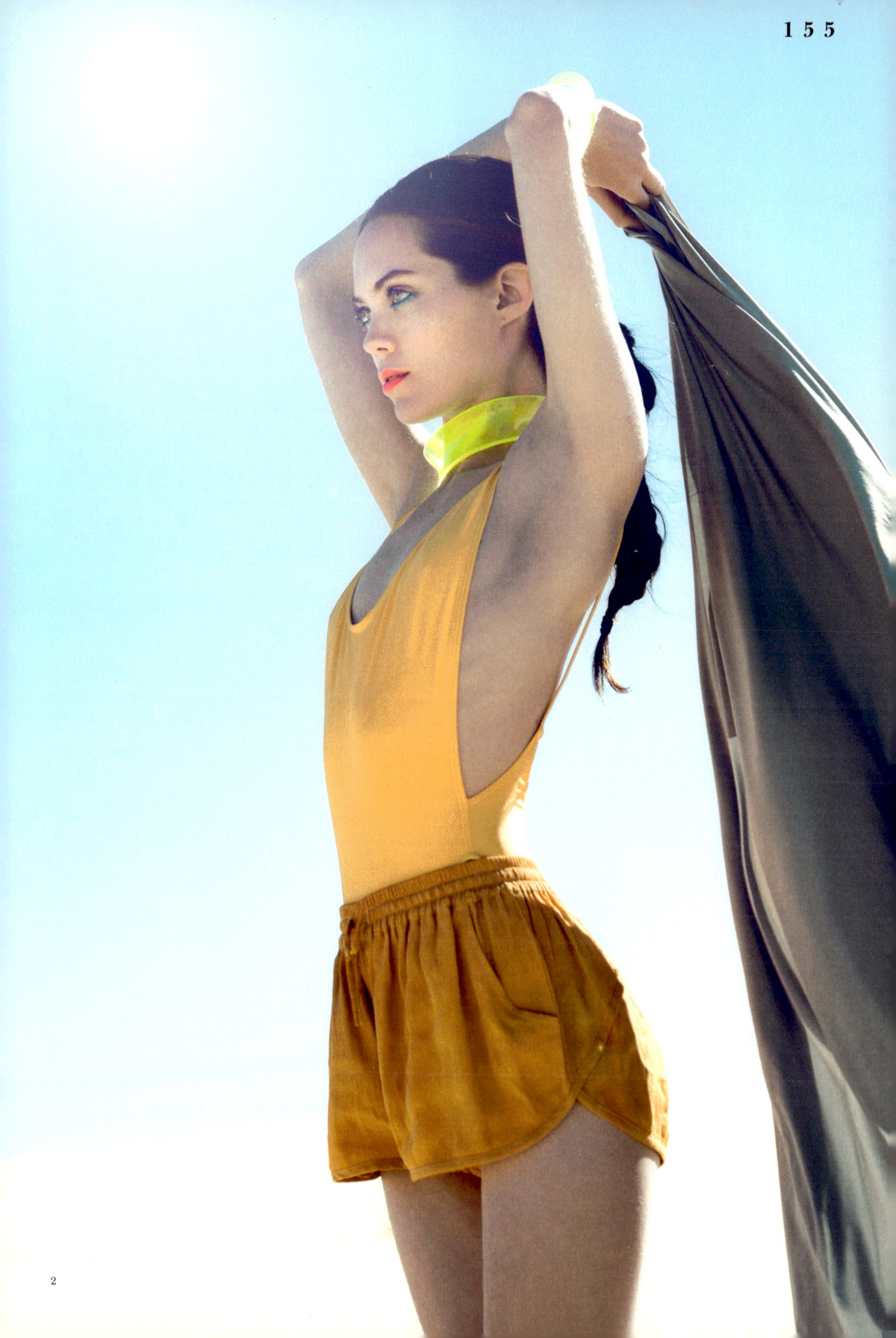

1

2

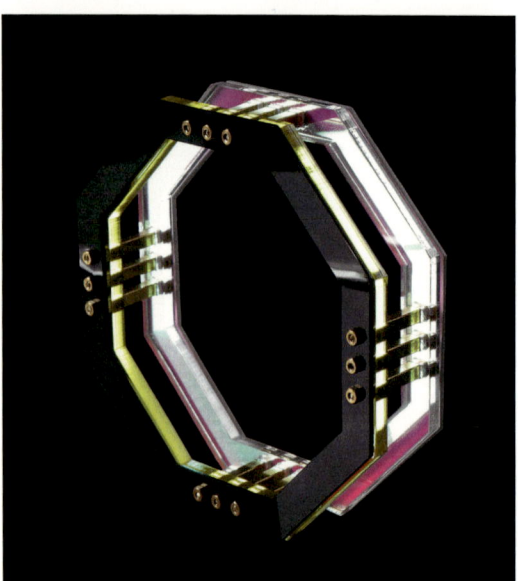

3

4

SARAH ANGOLD
"ACIES NECKLACE" [1]
"CETRA BRACELET" [2]
"QUEUS BRACELET" [3]
"IACIO EARRINGS" [4]
"VIA BRACELET" [5]

The futuristic, laser-cut acrylic jewelry by multidisciplinary design studio Sarah Angold make an
impact with their translucence, radiance, and colors.—
Laser-cut acrylic bracelet, magnetic fastenings—

1

MERLE O'GRADY
"DARKWING NECKLACE & BULLET EARRINGS" [1]

Merle O'Grady makes use of perspex laser cut into bold
geometric shapes, spikes, chunky vintage chains and
semi-precious gemstones to create an alluring blend of
punk industrialism and art deco.—Laser-cut black
gloss perspex, vintage 1960's brass chain, onyx nuggets,
Swarovski crystal, 24 karat gold-plated brass—

"AUTOMATON EARRINGS" [2]

—Laser-cut black gloss perspex, Swarovski crystal,
24 karat gold-plated brass—

RHEANNA LINGHAM
"GOLD EMBROIDERED NECKLACE"

Often using an eclectic mix of materials such as feathers, metals, and porcelain in her jewelry, Rheanna Lingham crafts her regal *Wheat Sheaf* necklace from intricately embroidered gold wire backed with leather.
—Gold wire, leather, gold-plated chain—

1

2

INA.SEIFART
"SCHIFFCHEN" [1]
Ina Seifart's lighthearted creations are based on objets
trouvés that are transformed into modern accessories. While some pieces use actual vintage objects
such as matchbox cars or spools of thread, others
are replicas that have been handcrafted in gold-plated
metal by the artist herself.—Paper with gold foil,
ring steel—

KIM BUCK
"SPELL IT OUT" [2]
See description on p. 164—750 gold—

1

KAT & BEE
"EMILIA" [1]

Kat Barry, the designer behind Kat & Bee, describes
her style as "contemporary and chaotic." A variety
of elements, such as precious stones, beads, and often
her trademark skull, are bound together by gold-
filled wire into daring one-off rings—14 karat gold
filled wire, selection of beads, 14 karat gold
filled bi-cones—

BYAMT INC.
"CONVERSATION STARTER NECKLACES" [2]

Conversation Starter by Alissia Melka-Teichroew adds
a thought-provoking and playful twist to the notion
of a statement necklace. Each set comes with three
stainless steel necklaces of diminishing legibility.
The necklaces are available in two texts—"This Is a
Secret" and "I Am Not Telling."—Silver-plated
stainless steel (Original in: Sterling silver, hand cut)—

KIM BUCK
"SOLITAIRE RING"

Kim Buck fashions wearable
pieces that offer reflections
on the form, meaning, and material
of jewelry. His pieces, often made
of gold, silver, and even metallic
foil, reference conventional design
concepts while simultaneously
deconstructing the same conventions.––750 gold––

"GOLD HEART"
––750 gold––

"GOLD BRACELET"
––Inflatable metallic plastic foil––

LAZY OAF
"PIZZA NECKLACE"
"JAZZY HAND NECKLACE"
"THE BOSS NECKLACE"
The jewelry line of this pop graphic design label from
London presents playful, candy-colored patterns
on printed perspex, enamel pendants, hairpieces, and
more.––Enamel––

LE BUISSON
"ÉQUALISEUR"
See description on p. 167––Pendant: 18 karat yellow
gold (17.40 gr), peridot, quartz, citrine garnet
(16.66 karat); Chain: yellow gold (3.20 gr), signed
and numbered piece ––

ALBEIT JEWELRY
"LETTERS"
Letters of the alphabet, numbers, and symbols drape
delicately across the wearer's neck in this line
of handcrafted pendant necklaces. The essence of the
design of the Albeit collection by Jenny Lu derives
from a cantilever in motion. The solid gold pendant
hangs horizontally from a gold chain at different
vertex points to achieve the most balanced composi-
tion possible, while also enabling the necklace
to fall and shift into various positions upon the
neck.––14 karat solid gold––

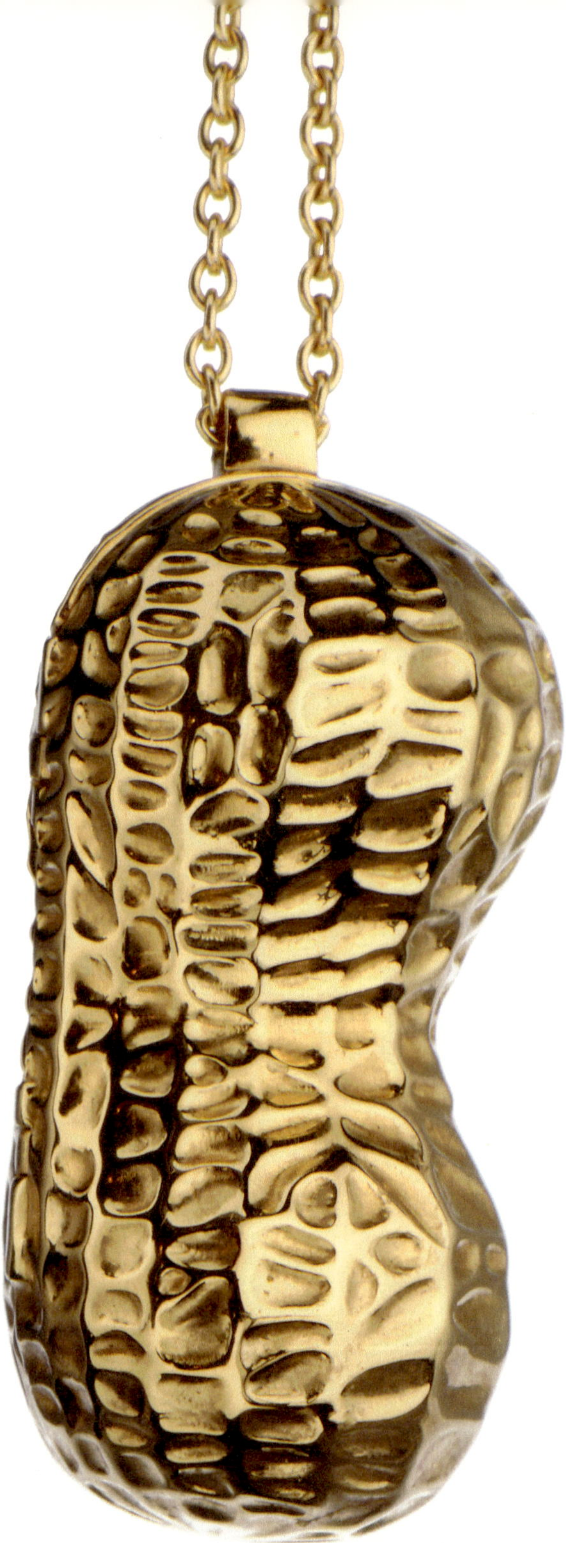

LE BUISSON
"PEANUT"
See description on p. 167—Pendant: 18 karat yellow
gold (21.80 gr), golden south sea pearls; Chain: yellow gold
(5.35 gr), length 50 cm, signed and numbered piece—

1

2

3

LE BUISSON
"THERMOKUKUS" [1]
Le Buisson, founded by Michele Monory, Francis
Fichot, Stéphane Arriubergé and Massimiliano Iorio,
works with various designers but in reality has
one main directive: to change the codes of jewelry.
Pendants in familiar, contemporary forms reveal
at second glance a lighthearted twist as joyful talis-
mans. Three jewelry collections have been realized
so far, designed by matali crasset, Geneviève Gauckler,
Mrzyk & Moriceau.—Pendant: 18 karat yellow gold
(15.20 gr), diamonds (0.22 karat)—

"UNE PATATE" [2]
—Pendant: 18 karat yellow gold (1.69 gr), diamonds
(0.01 karat)—

"TROIS PATATES" [3]
—Pendant: 18 karat yellow and white gold (5.49 gr),
diamonds (0.03 karat)—

1

2

3

4

JOANNA CAVE
"FISH" 1
Vintage jewelry, lace, and old black
and white photographs provide
the inspiration for the simple and
delicate jewelry by Joanna Cave.
The pieces are made from recycled
silver, which are then gold-plated
and occasionally embellished with
ethically sourced pearls.—Rose-
plated and oxidized silver. Japanese
Akoya Pearls—

"MARNI" 2
—Black rhodium, gold-plated
silver—

"MAGDALENNE" 3
—Rose- and gold-plated silver—

"THEANO" 4
—Gold- and rose-plated silver,
oxidized silver—

"KALYPSO" 5
—Rose-plated silver, oxidized
silver—

"VALERIE" 6
—Rose-plated silver. Japanese
Akoya Pearl—

"JOSIANE"

5

1

2

BELMACZ
"REQUIEM" [1]
The one-off and limited edition adornments by Julia
Muggenburg, the designer behind Belmacz, feature powerful and poetic combinations of earthy or
rare materials such as ebony, amber, fossilized
bone, pearls, or coral with fine metals.—Pearls, onyx,
18 karat yellow gold—

"POIRET PINS" [2]
—From left to right: Phosphosiderite, 18 karat yellow
gold; Grey moonstone, 18 karat yellow gold; Moonstone, 18 karat yellow gold; Marbeld grey agate, 18
karat yellow gold; Coral 18 karat, yellow gold; Bright
chrysoprase, 18 karat yellow gold—

THE OPULENT PROJECT
"RESIN EARRINGS" [3]
Founded by Meg Drinkwater and Erin Gardener,
TOP seeks to subvert mainstream preconceptions
regarding value in material culture. For their
Resin Earrings, silhouettes of royalty earrings were
dipped multiple times in resin and then set with
cubic zirconia, altering and obscuring their original
shape.—Resin, cubic zirconia, .925 silver—

KYOKO HASHIMOTO
"NU DECO PENDANT" [1]
Playfully ornamental, Kyoko Hashimoto's creations
combine metal with synthetic materials such
as acrylic, polyurethane, or sponge as their base.
Components are hand-dyed, and then hand-cut
or laser-cut, and then hand-finished in order
to achieve a special tactile quality.––Acrylic, brass,
sponge––

1

3

2

4

5

6

PIA ALEBORG
"IN THE ACT"

The starting point for this series of necklaces by Pia Aleborg was the typical Swedish suburb. Mundane details such as branches lying on the ground, repairs in the asphalt, and leaves lying in front yards are intuitively combined and translated into jewelry.

—1: Plywood, acrylic mirror, paint—

—2: Pink color, plywood—

—3: Plywood, silver-plated stick, green color, acrylic mirror—

—4: Teak, gray and green rubber—

—5: Plywood, drawing, stone, stick—

—6: Plywood, pink foam, drawing, gray rubber—

B Y A M T   I N C .
"JOINTED JEWELS" [1]

Jointed Jewels by Alissia Melka-Teichroew began as an exploration of ball joints and the unification of disparate elements as a single piece through selective laser sintering. The jewelry collection includes reference to classical jewelry icons, such as renaissance and Victorian creations, pieces by luxury brands Bulgari and Cartier, and even human bone structures.—3D printed polyamide (selective laser sintering technology)—

I N K A
"INKA KNOT" [2]

Made from sheer and soft nylon organza, the INKA collection by Katinka Fogh Vindelev was inspired by the bright colors used in ancient Indian jewelry, and also by the ability of fabric to be shaped, folded, tied, modeled, and puffed.—Rainbow red organza 100 % nylon, 14 carat gold-plated hook clasps and sewing thread—

1

1

2

RODRIGO ALMEIDA
"CALLIGRAPHY YELLOW"[1]

East meets West in Rodrigo Almeida's *Caligrafia* collection. In this series of bracelets and necklaces, calligraphy brushes that recall Asian writing traditions are juxtaposed with Western references such as Latin letters, and are interspersed with traditional beads.—Rope, gold pearls, precious rocks —

"CALLIGRAPHY BRACELET RED"[2]
—Rope, pearls, gold, wood—

GABRIEL & SCHWAN
"NECKLACE KNOT, BLUE"[3]

The chunky, sophisticated *Knot* necklace by design team Alex Gabriel and Fenke Schwan is crafted from nylon cord and bound by a silver clasp, and is available in a variety of eye-catching colors.—Nylon cord, silver—

3

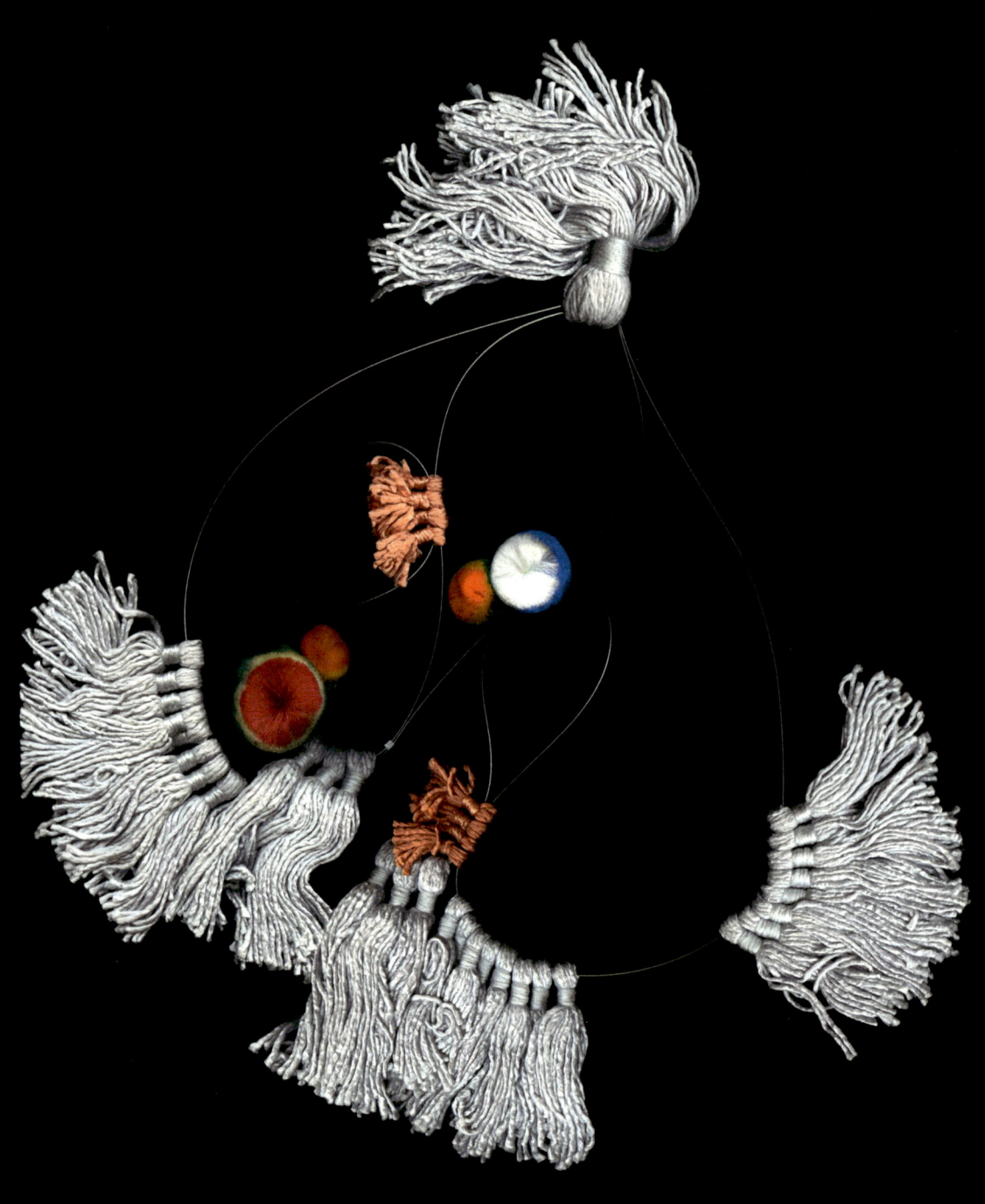

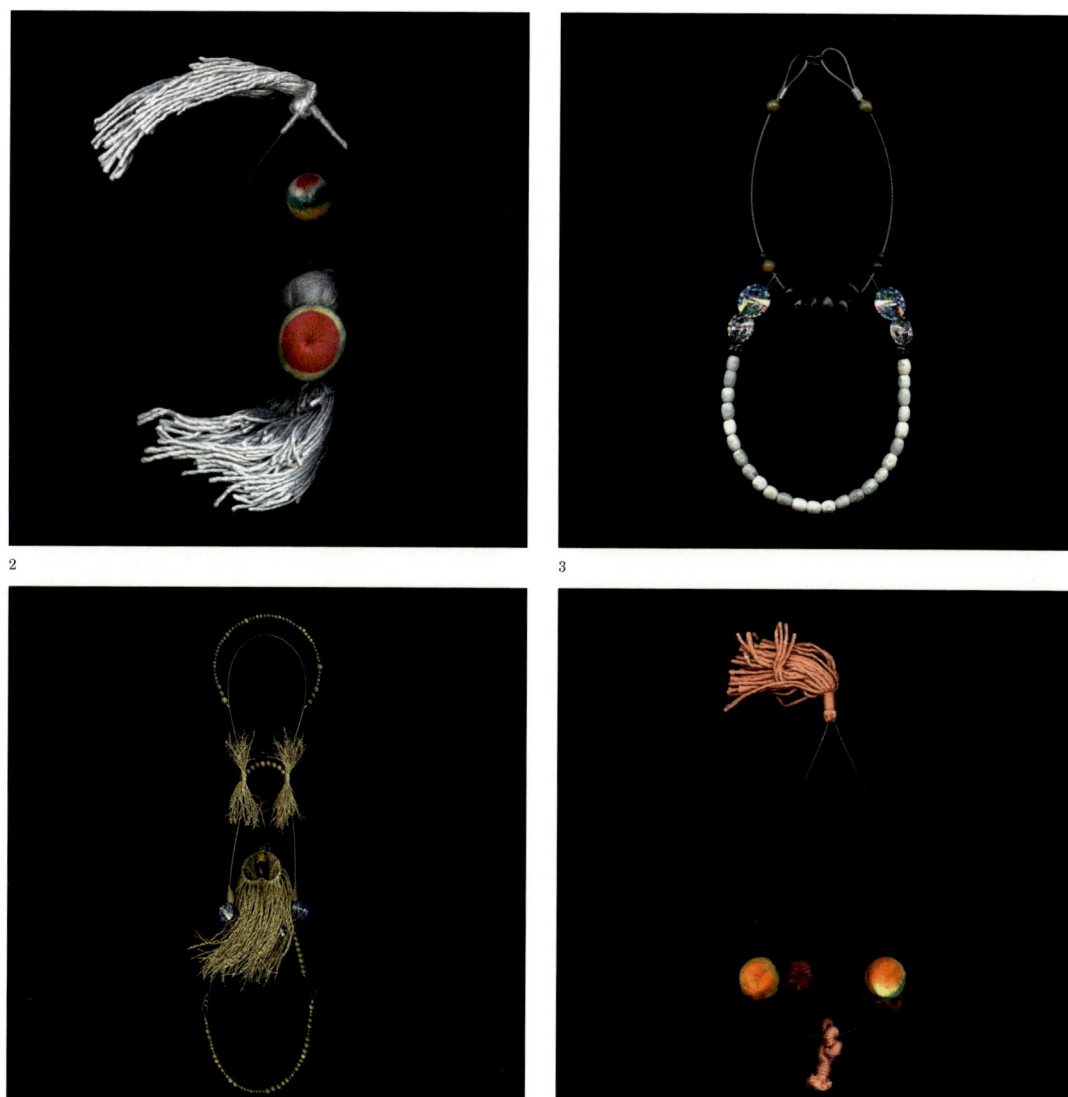

2

3

4

5

C C C H U
"CITY ROAMERS":
"BODICE" [1]
"POMPOM EARTH" [2]
"BALANCE OUT" [5]

Husband and wife duo Ching Ching and Michael
Chu describe the fashion and accessories they make
for women under their label CCCHU as "strong,
mysterious, lazy, and vigorous." Their textile-based
necklaces, featuring pom-poms or wooden beads
and seeds, reference traditional Chinese culture, while
the steel wire that holds them together signifies
the urban everyday.—Hand-dyed silk pompom, Indian
hand-dyed silk tassels, fine steel cable—

"AS A HUMAN BEING ON
EARTH" [3 & 4]

—Woods and seeds from bodhi tree, hemp twine,
Swarovski crystal, fine steel wire—

KELSEY QUAN
"CAMP ADVENTURES"
See description on p. 185—Agate stones, tie-dye
leather, rope and mesh cording, silk ombre ribbon,
magnetic clasp—

KELSEY QUAN
"CAMP ADVENTURES"

Kelsey Quan wraps and crochets an eclectic mix of
materials, such as agate amethyst and citrine rocks,
together with hand-painted snakeskin, hiking rope,
and neon cord to create statement necklaces invoking
tribal motifs with a colorful, urban twist.—Agate
stones, tie dye leather, rope and mesh cording, silk
ombre ribbon, magnetic clasp—

1

ALIKI STROUMPOULI
"TIGER" [1]

Inspired by the uncanny, Aliki Stroumpouli combines
diverse elements in her jewelry in order to sur-
prise and scandalize. In her *Recycling* series, she
created quirky and stylish one-off pieces from beads,
chains, and other elements left over from past
jewelry collections that would otherwise have gone
to waste. Her *Pearls and Beads* collection made
from ping-pong balls is further testament to her
panache for combining everyday materials
into wearable sculptures.—Beads, metallic parts—

"BLACK MIRROR (DETAIL)" [2]
—Beads, metallic parts, metallic chain—

1

2

3

DENISE JULIA REYTAN

"LIVING MEMORY" [1]

Denise Julia Reytan might be considered a modern bricoleur, as she combines a potpourri of found objects into colorful statement necklaces that she calls "poems on the body." Regardless of their market value, the diverse objects are equal in their symbolic value for their creator, who "harmonizes" them in materiality and color through silicone or silver casting—Reconstructed coral, real coral, rose quartz, silver—

"FRAICHE" [2]

—Amethyst, pearls, rubber, silicone, rose quartz, glass—

"VERREAUXII" [3]

—Carneol, coral, cairngorm, rose quartz, garnet, silver, stainless steel, silicone, plastic, rope—

"FRU1TS" [4]

—Silicone, plastic, ironwire, ribbon, lace—

4

1

2

3

4

5

ROARKE NEW YORK

"LE ROSE" 3

The soft necklaces by Laetitia Stanfield and Mignonne Gavigan of Roarke New York are a clear fusion of apparel and jewelry. Soft chiffon or tulle silk in a variety of colors and patterns is draped bib-like around the wearer's neck, and is adorned with hand-applied beads, pearls, studs, and other decoration.—Seed beads, silk chiffon—

"LE BUCI" 4

—Seed beads, silk chiffonsnap back closure—

"LE CHARLOT AZTEC" 2&5

—2: Glass seed beads, tulle, crepe satin, snap back closure—

—5: Seed beads, tulle, crepe satin, snap back closure—

"LE INCA" 6

—Seed beads, silk chiffon—

DENISE JULIA REYTAN

"FLYING ME" 1

—Amazonit, silicone, white agate, resin, plastic, rope, rose quartz, feather—

6

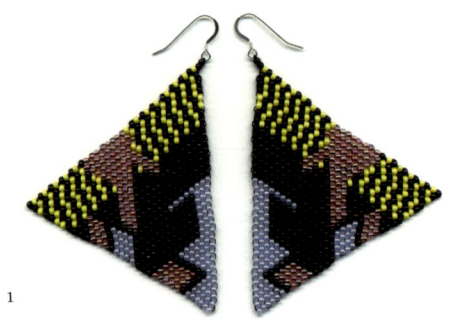

1

2

3

4

BROKENFAB

For her *Disco and Boogie Beading* collection,
Fabienne Morel of brokenfab uses the dance floor as
inspiration by stringing high-energy combinations
of Rocailles beads into colorful tribal designs,
producing geometric patterns and asymmetrical shapes.
In line with this club culture aesthetic, some
of the beads become fluorescent when exposed to UV
light.—5: Rocailles glass beads—

"PYRAMIDE EARRINGS" 1
—Rocailles glass beads—

"DISCO NECKLACE" 2
"ROCKET NECKLACE" 3
"FREESTYLE NECKLACE" 4
—Rocailles glass beads—

5

NAOKO OGAWA
"GATHERING JEWELRY"

Naoko Ogawa's *Gathering Jewelry* collection is truly
interactive. The wearer crushes aluminum sheets
of various color and size against his or her clothes
according to whim, adding new folds to the underlying
textiles in innumerable and unpredictable ways.
The jewelry—made manifest by way of a sensual
process of creation through destruction—is also
recyclable, as the artist encourages wearers to discard
the jewelry, not only due to the danger of sharp
edges and broken metal, but also to avoid it becoming
commonplace and thus making one's life stagnant.
—Aluminum, paper—

J O S H U A   S C O T T
"STACK SIGNS SERIES #4"
See description on p. 198

1

J O S H U A   S C O T T
"STACK SIGNS SERIES #1" [1]
"STACK SIGNS SERIES #2" [2]
In his *Stack Signs* photo series, Joshua Scott presents
a colorful mash-up: the bold creations by various
jewelry designers are merged with the street art form
of gang hand sign stacking, in a humorous comment
on the appropriation of street culture by the fashion
industry.—Credits: nOir Jewelry, La Cresia
Gloves, Vintage Costume Jewelry at New World Order
Boutiques NYC, Bijules Jewelry—

200

2

1

ARIELLE DE PINTO
"HINGED
SKULL NECKLACE" [1]

Featuring her trademark technique of hand-crocheted metal chains, Arielle de Pinto's collection of pendant necklaces integrates sculptural elements, such as brutalist, figurative cast figures, or geometric metal plates and inlaid stones invoking art deco influences. De Pinto also tries to avoid the use of prefabricated elements, such as clasps, preferring continuous necklaces or the use of hand-carved clasps and hinges.—Red e-coat brass, 925 sterling silver—

"LINK CLUSTER NECKLACE" [2]
—Palladium-plated brass, 925 sterling silver—

"STIFF LADY NECKLACE" [3]
—Palladium-plated brass, 925 sterling silver—

"MAN SITTING LADY NECKLACE" [4]
—Palladium-plated brass, 925 sterling silver—

3

4

ZELDA
BEAUCHAMPET
"MR. NECKLESS"

The playful *Mr. Neckless* necklace
collection by Zelda Beauchampet
is reminiscent of the children's toy Mr.
Potato Head. The necklace is based
on various combinations of three
different noses, hairstyles, mustaches,
and glasses, each available in seven
different colors. —Silver, acrylic—

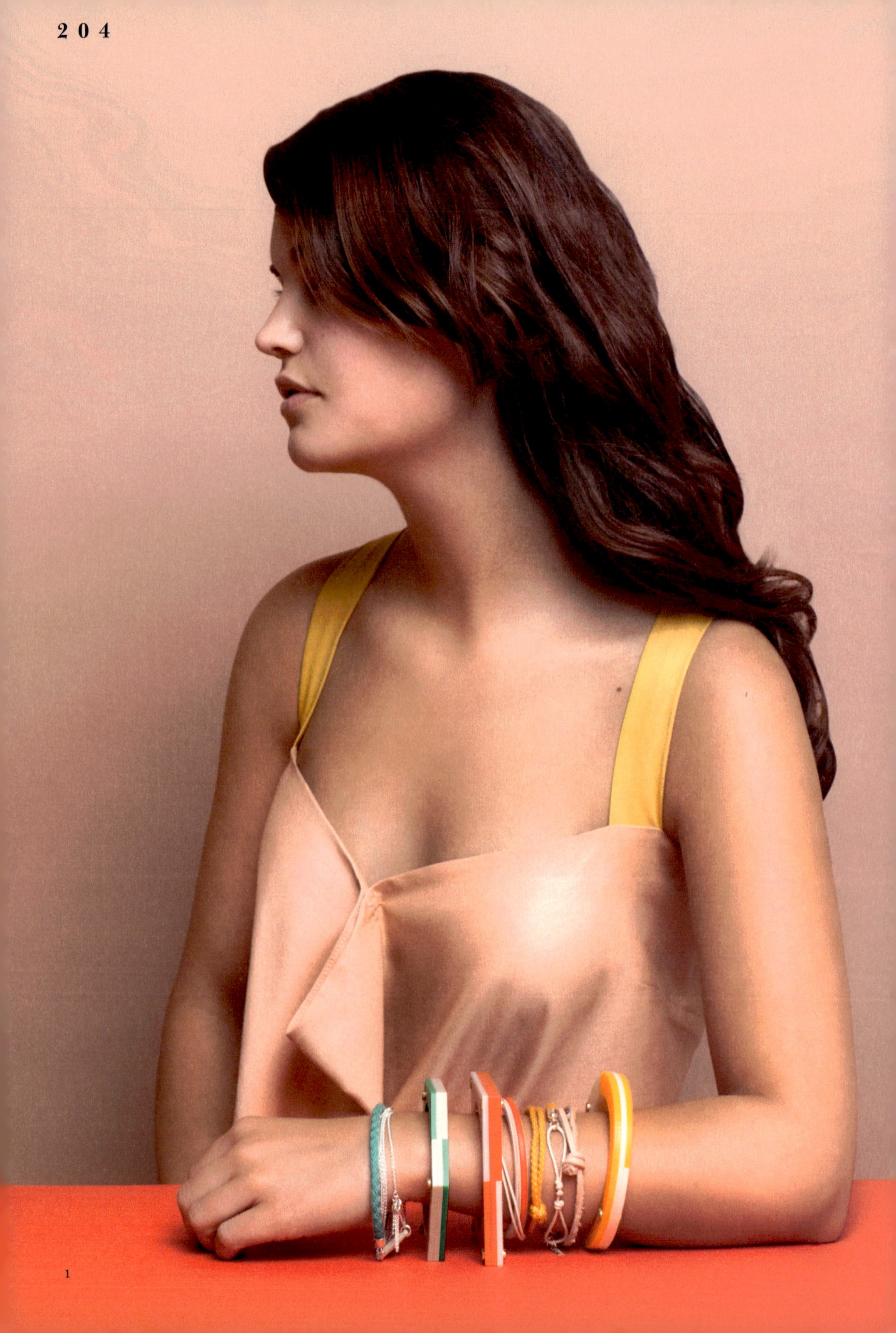

1

2

ZELDA BEAUCHAMPET
"THE BOYSCOUTS"
Zelda Beauchampet's collection *The Boyscouts* combines urban and outdoor materials and iconic shapes into jewelry and fashion accessories that are understated yet upbeat.—1: Silver, wood, acrylic, leather, cotton—2: Silver, wood, acrylic, leather, cotton—

NOON PASSAMA X EK
"ETHNIC—PART I–IV"
The collaborative project by jewelry designer
Noon Passama and fashion designer Ek Thongprasert
investigates notions of preciousness. Enlarged
silhouettes of classical western and eastern ethnic jewelry are enlarged and cast in silicone or brass,
preserving the original contours but homogenizing the
colors and materials. In more recent pieces from
this ongoing project, the multifaceted brass
models are covered with dyed fur and accentuated
with gold or copper plating.—Silicone—

NOON PASSAMA X EK
"ETHNIC—PART I–IV"
—See description on p. 206—

—1: Horse skin, brass, car paint—

—2: Horse skin, black rhodium-plated brass—

1

WILLEMIJN DE GREEF
"TRADITIONS,
HALSSIERAAD ZEEUWSE
KNOPE" [1]
See description on p. 79—Silver, brown and black
porcelain, thread—

"CUFF LINKS
ZEEUWSE KNOPEN" [2]
—Silver—

2

2

3

U L I
"ELIZABETH" [1]
Inspired by Elizabethan jewelry and principles of
trompe l'oeil, Designer Uli Rapp opens up a dialogue
on bling with her oversized and screenprinted
diamond and pearl necklaces and layered gold chains.
The prints are done on a unique combination of
layered tricot and rubber that Rapp developed herself,
while the use of various metallic inks lends the
pieces particular shine and depth.—Textile, rubber,
screenprinting—

"FACETTES" [2] & "CHAINS RE" [3]
—Textile, rubber, screenprinting, foil—

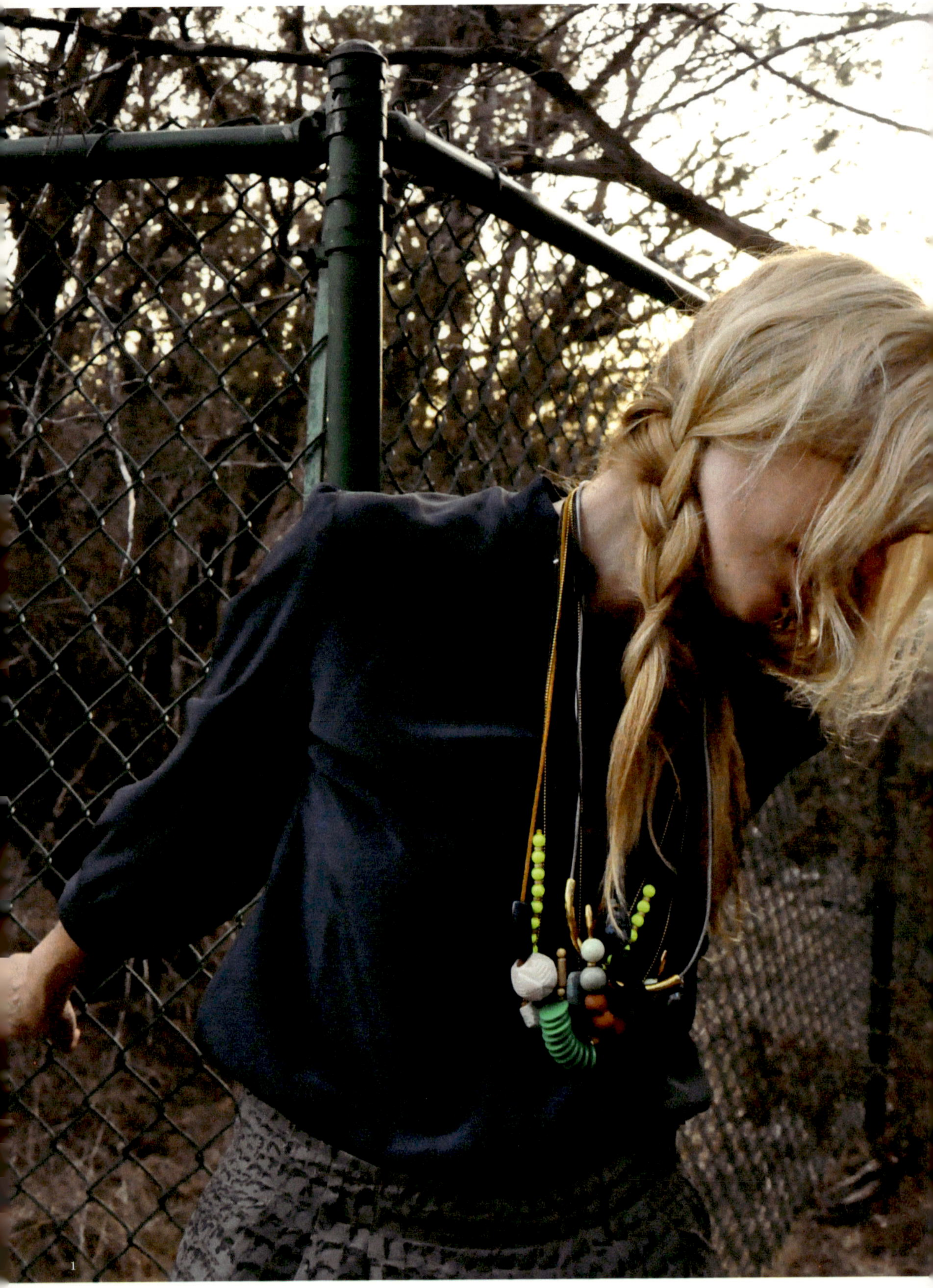
1

2

ALYSON FOX
"A SMALL COLLECTION" [1]
The jewelry creations by Alyson Fox are lessons in
joyful understatement. Delicate leather bands
and chains join colorful vintage beads in Lucite and
plastic, brass, or wood into dangling necklaces
designed to be layered or worn alone.—Vintage beads,
leather, chain, brass and cotton cording—

"A SMALL COLLECTION" [2]
—Vintage beads, wood on leather, woven cording—

ARIELLE DE PINTO
"HAIRY MINI POUCH"

Arielle de Pinto uses the traditional technique of crochet to weave metal threads of silver and gold into intricate, loose structures that can be worn as necklaces, bracelets, gloves, and body sheaths. The weight of the metal allows each piece to drape differently over the individual body of the wearer.— Stainless steel, ionized stainless steel, 925 sterling silver, palladium-plated 925 sterling silver—

MARQUIS & CAMUS
"BOWTIE NECKLACE"
See description on p. 223—Vintage bow tie,
mixed chain—

APRÈS SKI
"ARQUITECTURE" [1 & 4]
Golden brass and resin pieces are combined by Après
Ski designer Lucia Vergara with beads or fabrics
culled from the 1940s to the 1980s to create geometric
pendants in playful, vintage aesthetic.—Resin, brass—

"COSMIC ICE CREAM":
"LYNX" [2] & "CORONA AUSTRALIS" [3]
—Vintage centerpiece, gold brass chain—

1

2

ELIZABETH KNIGHT
"LONG STACKED NECKLACE" [1]
"STACKED NECKLACE" [2]
"TUBE NECKLACE" [3 & 4]

Elizabeth Knight's metallic jewelry plays with a primitive, handmade aesthetic, often taking inspiration from forms in nature. For her recent collection *Primitive*, the designer translates tribal iconography—whose originals might be in bone, rope, or stone—into elegant creations in brass and leather.—Brass, leather—

3

4

1

2

MARQUIS & CAMUS
"BUTTON NECKLACE" [1]

Marquis & Camus, founded by designer Sarah Kang, hearkens back to a more romantic era while remaining rooted in the present. Vintage elements such as chandelier crystals, charms, and buttons are brought together with contemporary elements including metallic chains, hand-died ribbons, rhinestones, and pearls to create whimsical creations with a classic twist.—Copper plates, brass rings, gold burnish chain, brass clasp—

"PRINCESS'S
CROWN NECKLACE" [2]

—Vintage brass frame and glass cameo, crystal crown, brass button and glass studs, rhinestone chain, grosgrain ribbon, vintage Japanese clasp—

MARQUIS & CAMUS
"CHAINMAIL BODY NECKLACE"
See description on p. 223—Brass frame and
rings, crystals, gold burnish chain, brass chain—

TJEP.
"WINGS"

The *Clockwork Love* series of pendants by design
group Tjep. deals with notions of love and time.
Numerous thematically related graphics cut from
paper or gold-plated metal are arranged, layer
for layer, into delicate mechanical arrangements.
The subthemes "Peace," "Evil," and "Black Bling" use
the same method of cutting and layering analo-
gous graphics.—Acrylic, paper—

1

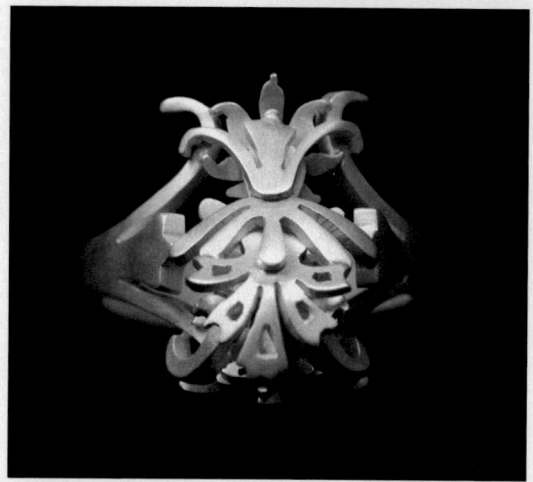

2

3

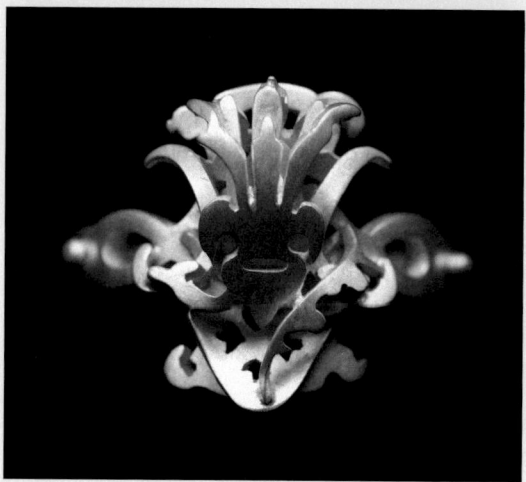

4

GITTE NYGAARD
"ORNAMENT AND CRIME" [1]
"ORNAMENT IS HIGH ART HIDDEN EVERYWHERE (EVERYWHERE)" [2]
"ORNAMENT IS HIGH ART HIDDEN EVERYWHERE (HIGH)" [3]
"ORNAMENT IS HIGH ART HIDDEN EVERWHERE (ORNAMENT)" [4]

In this collection, Gitte Nygaard takes the ornamentation of the Bodoni font to transform text into jewelry, making a critical yet humorous comment on the early modernist denunciation of decoration as empty abundance. Using the *Bodoni Ornaments Keystroke Guide* as her reference, in which each ornament corresponds to a letter of the alphabet, the artist makes words and sentences from her creations.—Silver—

1

2

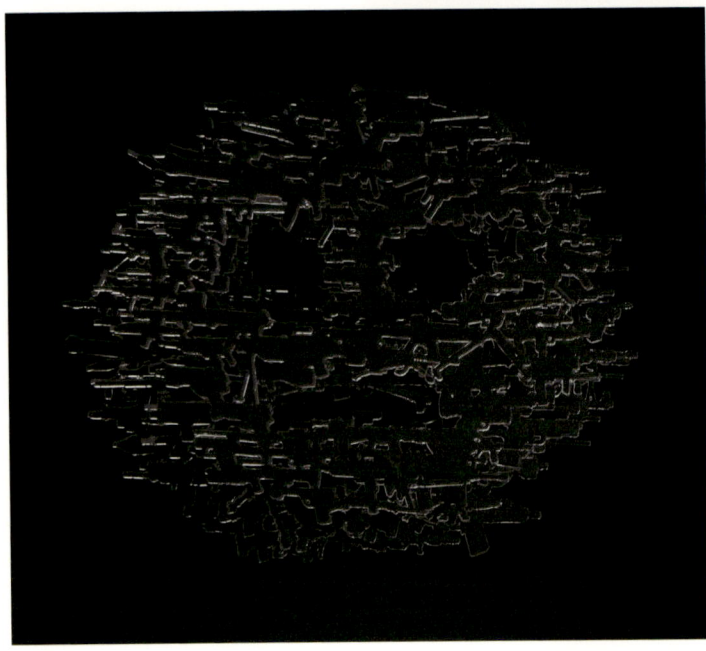

3

NERVOUS SYSTEM
"HYPHAE RING" [1&4]
"HYPHAE BROOCH" [2]

Nervous System develops mathematical algorithms and interactive systems to create computer-generated patterns that are reminiscent of natural phenomena, such as cellular structures and rhizome-like networks, which they then translate into jewelry. Designs are 3D laser printed in nylon as the final product, or set in wax to create molds from which to cast metal models, or cut directly onto wool or silicone rubber.—3D-printed nylon—

TJEP.
"EVIL" [3]

See description on p. 226—
Acrylic, paper—

4

INDEX

A

ADI ZAFFRAN WEISLER
"BULLET RING"
2010—Edition: 1—*p. 84*
www.adizaffran.com Tel Aviv-Yafo, Israel

●

AKONG LONDON
"GOLD LEAF BRACELET"
2010—Edition: Multiple—*p. 20*

—

"CHAIN HARNESS"[1]
"GOLD LEAF NECKLACE"[2]
2010—Edition: Multiple—*pp. 24, 25*

—

"CRYSTAL TASSEL COLLAR"[1]
"BRIGHT POM POM NECKLACE"[2]
2011—*pp. 44, 45*
Designer: Nicole Akong
www.akonglondon.com London, UK

●

ALBEIT JEWELRY
"LETTERS"
Designer: Jenny Lu—2009—Edition: Alphabets
A–Z—Photo: Steven Hong—*p. 165*
www.albeitjewelry.com Los Angeles, USA

●

ALEXANDRA BLAK
"YASMIN EARRING"[1]
2010—Edition: 50—Photo: Zanita Morgan—*p. 154*

—

"MADAME NEON CHOKER"[2]
2011—Edition: 50—*p. 155*
Designer: Alexandra Anson
www.alexandrablak.com.au Melbourne, Australia

●

ALIKI STROUMPOULI
"TIGER"[1]
"BLACK MIRROR (DETAIL)"[2]
2008—Edition: 1—Photo: Aliki Stroumpouli—*pp. 186, 187*
www.alikistroumpouli.com Athens, Greece

●

ALYSON FOX
"OBJECT 3"
Brand/Client: A Small Collection by
Alyson Fox–2009—*p. 33*

—

"A SMALL COLLECTION"[1]
2011—Edition: 45 of each necklace—Photo:
Alyson Fox—*p. 214*

—

"A SMALL COLLECTION"[2]
2011—Edition: 30 of each necklace—*p. 215*

—

"OBJECT 1"[1]
"OBJECT 4"[2]
Brand/Client: A Small Collection by Alyson
Fox—2009—Edition: 1—*p. 138*
www.alysonfox.com Austin, USA

●

ANDREA AUER
"KULTURPERLEN"[1]
2007—Photo: Daniela Beranek—*p. 100*

—

"THE WHITE TUBE"[2]
2010—Edition: 1—Photo: Daniela Beranek—*p. 101*
www.andreaauer.at Vienna, Austria

●

ANTIATOMS
"BIG LEATHER BROOCH"[1]
2005—Edition: 25—Photo: ANTIATOMS—*p. 95*

—

"LEATHER NECKLACE"[2]
2005—Edition: 15—Photo: Lionel Malka—*p. 95*
www.antiatoms.com Madrid, Spain

●

AOI KOTSUHIROI
"FLOATING SHADOWS"[1]
"DAY DREAM"[2]
"ENDLESS"[3]
"NAKED SOLITUDE"[4]
2011—Edition: Unique/One-off piece—Photo:
Aoi Kotsuhiroi—*pp. 128, 129*

—

"SLEEPING SHADOW"[1]
"ALL SORTS OF RAINS"[2]
2011—Edition: Unique/One-off piece—
Photo: Aoi Kotsuhiroi—*pp. 130, 131*
www.aoikotsuhiroi.com France

●

APRÈS SKI
"ARQUITECTURE"[1 & 4]
2011—Photo: David Urbano—*p. 218, 219*

—

"COSMIC ICE CREAM—LYNX"[2]
"COSMIC ICE CREAM—CORONA
AUSTRALIS"[3]
2011—Edition: 1—*p. 219*
www.apresskishop.com Barcelona, Spain

●

ARIELLE DE PINTO
"HINGED SKULL
NECKLACE"[1]
"LINK CLUSTER NECKLACE"[2]
"STIFF LADY NECKLACE"[3]
"MAN SITTING LADY NECKLACE"[4]
2009—*pp. 200, 201*

—

"HAIRY MINI POUCH"
2011—Photo: George Barberis—*p. 216*
www.arielledepinto.com Montreal, Canada

●

ARMOR JEWELRY
"ABEE"[1]
"CHRISTOPHE"[2]
Designer: Sandee Shin—2010—Photo: Jason
Banker—*pp. 60, 61*
www.armorjewelry.com New York, USA

●

ATELIER TED NOTEN
"ICE NECKLACE"
2007—Photo: Atelier Ted Noten—*p. 17*

A GIRL'S BEST FRIENDS

Creative Jewelry Design

EDITED by Robert Klanten, Sven Ehmann

TEXT AND PREFACE by Alisa Anh Kotmair

COVER by Daniela Burger and Floyd Schulze for Gestalten
COVER PHOTOGRAPHY by Maxime Ballesteros,
Jewelry by Denise J. Reytan, Model: Jill Ankawi/Satory MGMT
LAYOUT by Daniela Burger for Gestalten
TYPEFACES Hellschreiber Sans by Joerg Schmitt,
www.gestaltenfonts.com; New Century Schoolbook by Morris Fuller Benton,
Matthew Carter; Bulmer MT by Morris Fuller Benton

PROJECT MANAGEMENT by Vanessa Diehl for Gestalten
PRODUCTION MANAGEMENT by Janine Milstrey for Gestalten
PROOFREADING by Transparent Language Solutions
PRINTED by Eberl Print, Immenstadt/Allgäu

Bibliographic information published by the Deutsche
Nationalbibliothek. The Deutsche Nationalbibliothek
lists this publication in the Deutsche Nationalbiblio-
grafie; detailed bibliographic data are available online
at http://dnb.d-nb.de.

None of the content in this book was published in
exchange for payment by commercial parties or
designers; Gestalten selected all included work based
solely on its artistic merit.

This book was printed according to the internationally
accepted ISO 14001 standards for environmental
protection, which specify requirements for an environmental management system.

This book was printed on paper certified by the FSC®.

Gestalten is a climate-neutral company. We col-
laborate with the non-profit carbon offset provider
myclimate (www.myclimate.org) to neutralize the
company's carbon footprint produced through our
worldwide business activities by investing in projects
that reduce CO_2 emissions (www.gestalten.com/
myclimate).

Made in Germany
Published by Gestalten, Berlin 2012
ISBN 978-3-89955-418-2